BASICS

FASHION DESIGN

Developing
a Fashion Collection

Second Edition

Fairchild Books
An imprint of Bloomsbury Publishing Plc

B L O O M S B U R Y
LONDON · OXFORD · NEW YORK · NEW DELHI · SYDNEY

Fairchild Books

An imprint of Bloomsbury Publishing Plc

Imprint previously known as AVA Publishing

50 Bedford Square
London
WC1B 3DP
UK

1385 Broadway
New York
NY 10018
USA

www.bloomsbury.com

FAIRCHILD BOOKS, BLOOMSBURY and
the Diana logo are trademarks of Bloomsbury
Publishing Plc

First published 2016

British Library Cataloguing-in-Publication Data
A catalogue record for this book is available from
the British Library.

ISBN:
PB: 978-2-9404-9673-0
ePDF: 978-1-4725-3914-4

Library of Congress Cataloging-in-Publication Data
Renfrew, Elinor.
Developing a fashion collection / Elinor Renfrew
and Colin Renfrew.—Second edition.
pages cm.—(Basic fashion design)
ISBN 978-2-940496-73-0 (paperback)
—ISBN 978-1-4725-3914-4 (ePDF)
—ISBN 978-2-940496-56-3 (ePUB)
1. Fashion design. 2. Fashion. 3. Fashion
designers—Interviews. 4. Fashion shows.
I. Renfrew, Colin. II. Title.
TT507.R44 2016
746.9'2—dc23
2015008462

Cover Image: Zoe Wells, Kingston University
Collection line up 2014
Design by Evelin Kasikov
Printed and bound in China

://neo:trib

A/W '

Lucinda Popp final
collection line-up, Kingston
University, A/W 2014

Introduction
007

Chapter 1

What Is a Collection?
009
How to Start a Collection
011
Market Research
012
Inspiration
018
Development
022
Fabric Sourcing
024
Forecasting Trends
026
Archiving
028
Editing Collections
029
The Team
030
Showing the Collection
036

Interviews:
Martin Raymond, The
Future Laboratory
042
Shelley Fox
044
Holly Fulton
046
Todd Lynn
048
Richard Nicoll
050
Felipe Rojas Llanos
052

Chapter 2

**Collections and Their
Influences**
055
Background
056
Historical
058
Cultural
060
Conceptual
062
Functional
065
Political
068
Futuristic
070
Artistic
072

Interviews:
Fiona Stuart, Rellik
074
Lou Amendola, Brooks
Brothers
076
Dr Noki
078
Katie Greenyer, Red or
Dead
080
Sophie Hulme
082
Kenneth MacKenzie, Six
Eight Seven Six
084
Will Broome
086

Chapter 3

**Designing for Different
Markets**
089
Haute Couture
090
Ready-to-Wear
094
Designer Labels
096
Luxury Brands
099
Designer Collaborations
100
High Street
102
Developing High-Street
Collections
104
Online Shopping
106

Interviews:
Giles Deacon
108
Sibling
110
Colin McNair, John
Varvatos
112
Gordon Richardson,
Topman
114
John Mooney
116

Chapter 4

Specialist Collections
119
Childrenswear
120
Knitwear
122
Active Sportswear
124
Corporate Wear
125
Footwear, Bags, and
Accessories
126

Interviews:
Eva Karayiannis, Caramel
Baby & Child
128
Sam Leutton, Leutton
Postle
132
Charli Cohen
134
Tracy Mulligan,
People Tree
136
Nicholas Kirkwood
138
Oliver Ruuger
140

Chapter 5

The Student Collection
143
The Brief
144
Your Portfolio
151
Research and Development
154
Presentation
162
Conclusion
168

Index
170
Shops and Markets
174
Suppliers
178
**Fashion Weeks, Trade
Shows, and Fabric Fairs**
180
**Fashion Journals,
Museums, and Blogs**
182
**Acknowledgments and
Picture Credits**
184

Introduction

All designers go through the same stages when developing a collection. Whether they have their own label or are employed by a large company, the starting point and processes are invariably the same: research, design, development, editing, and presentation.

Developing a Fashion Collection (Second Edition) guides you through the different aspects of the development process. The first chapter asks "What is a collection?" and covers the starting points including initial research, trend, color, and fabric, as well as exploring the different roles within the team involved in developing a collection. **Chapter 2** looks at the common themes used by designers for research, including historical, political, global, and environmental influences. **Chapter 3** introduces different types of collections, looking at market level, from ready-to-wear to online shopping.

Chapter 4 covers collections designed for niche markets, including knitwear and fair trade, and finally **Chapter 5** provides an invaluable summary of the process of developing a student collection.

Developing a Fashion Collection (Second Edition) is richly illustrated with up-to-the-moment images from international collections, both on and off the catwalk, as well as archive images. Underpinning each chapter are exclusive interviews with designers from all over the fashion industry, who share their own experiences of developing collections.

1   **Louis Vuitton, S/S 2013 by Marc Jacobs.**

1

What is a collection?

Designed and produced for sale—either through retailers or direct to customers—a collection is a range of garments, accessories, or products brought together to tell a story. This range of pieces may be inspired by a trend, theme, or design direction, reflecting cultural and social influences, and is usually designed for a season or particular occasion. A collection is a grouping of outfits or looks presented in a variety of ways, from catwalk presentations at one of the international fashion weeks to online web pages. Collections, which can include mainline (which is seasonal), pre-collection, diffusion, resort, and cruise, are aimed at different levels of the market and represent a designer's vision and signature. This chapter introduces the concept of the collection and the processes involved in its development.

1   Celine, A/W 2013.

2 Burberry, A/W 2014.
Womenswear finale.

HOW TO START A COLLECTION

Any successful or financially viable collection requires an enormous amount of research, investigation, and planning. Successful designers, manufacturers, and retailers have a clear understanding of their customers' needs, as well as an understanding of their position in a highly competitive market. In addition to the creation and realization of any collection, designers need to consider a range of issues if the final garments are to hang in customers' closets.

If we look back at designers who have influenced fashion with their collections, all have one thing in common: an obsessive belief in their vision for a collection that represents their aesthetic and tells a story.

Collections also need to make a strong statement in order to inspire the press and the customers. This statement can range from a romantic, historical narrative to a modern, minimalistic collection based simply on clever use of geometrics or color.

Designers are increasingly producing pre-collections, in addition to the main seasonal collections, in order to generate more sales; they are also introducing smaller more specific collections, such as resort, derived from the main collection. For example, a designer for a design house in Paris will be expected to design up to ten collections a year. At Chanel there will be two haute couture, two ready-to-wear, two pre-collections, a cruise, and special collections for charity events, with anything from 20 to 120 looks per collection. Designers will often have the same again for their own label.

MARKET RESEARCH

Designing a collection involves research within two distinct areas: inspirational and market research. In order to gain an understanding of current fashion stock and ranges across market levels, many, if not all, designers will conduct a *comp shop*. This term refers to comparing stock in competitor retail outlets, regardless of market level. Quality of fabric, construction, and detailing are carefully studied alongside prices and origin of manufacturing. This provides a great deal of information that is useful when planning and selling a fashion collection. If it is not the first collection, market research involves looking back at what has sold well, comparing with competitors, and analyzing why the customer will buy a certain product or pieces from a particular designer or brand.

Designers in larger companies will liaise with buyers and merchandisers to ensure that their creative vision is represented within the cost. Ultimately, it will be the fashion buyers who make the decision to order fashion ranges, and their decisions are based on a combination of the following: historical knowledge of their particular customers; sales figures, which track how many items of each piece within the collection were bought the previous season; delivery and availability of stock; quality of merchandise; exclusivity; and price.

Many small fashion businesses lack the infrastructure to access accurate market and marketing information. However, intuition and awareness of fashion directions will help a start-up label become commercially successful. Buyers are usually cautious when adopting new designers and therefore use a system of sale or return, which offers new talent the opportunity to showcase their collections alongside more established brands; they can then be picked up as the next new name if their collections sell.

Another way of launching a new fashion business is by concentrating on one particular piece. Many successful designers have started this way, later expanding into a range of product areas based on their hero product. Calvin Klein's first collection was a range of women's coats, for example; Ralph Lauren began his vast empire with a small collection of ties; and Laura Ashley started her global business with a humble printed tea towel.

3   Ralph Lauren menswear at the opening of the flagship store in Bloomingdale's.

What is a collection?

Market research

Identifying the customer

By careful investigation and competitor analysis, designers can begin to identify a specific market area and customer for their fashion vision. At times, designers will create an imaginary situation where characters are involved in a plot, journey, or scenario. Characters may be well-known historical figures or completely fictitious, but this collage of people and events can provide a rich starting point for imagining, visualizing, and defining colors, fabrics, and shapes without constraints. Although this makes for a romantic or stylized approach to customer profiling, most large companies are able to define every aspect of their customers through sales and specialist marketing information.

This information takes into account social and economic influences and how customers' lives are defined by a range of factors. Successful fashion producers are able to define their customers in relation to the business, from the past and present to the future. It is possible to start with a fashion view, or purist approach to fashion, where an aspect of the process— perhaps creative cutting—informs the final pieces. The customer, occasion, and cost remain considerations if the final garments are to work in any commercial context. However, not all pieces within a collection are designed on a commercial basis. Catwalk showpieces work as a promotional tool to attract the press, which helps to reinforce the designer's popularity and currency.

4   John Galliano. A collage of people and events can provide a rich starting point for imaging, visualizing, and defining colors, fabrics, and shapes without constraints.

Market research

"Creativity is a
subjective issue,
as all fashion
expresses a creative
vision and process."

Creativity versus wearability

Creativity is a subjective issue, as all fashion
expresses a creative vision and process.
Wearability is also subjective and rests with
the consumer, who can make personal
judgments about self-image, acceptability,
and suitability, depending on occasion or
lifestyle. Today's consumer is inundated with
fashion choices, and the media's infatuation
with fashion, celebrity, and influence provides
enormous coverage of how fashion and style
can be portrayed.

Many designers will create extravagant
showpieces—whether they are hats,
shoes, or garments—which are deliberately
included to excite the fashion press and
gain maximum coverage. Established
fashion houses stage catwalk shows for
both haute couture and ready-to-wear,
and designers are encouraged to create
spectacular, theatrical shows as a prelude
to the advertising campaigns. Showpieces
are often the result of creative collaboration.

Alexander McQueen, for example,
collaborated with Milliner Philip Treacy to
enhance their catwalk statements. This type
of collection is more about storytelling than
sales. Other designers are innovative in the
way they present their collections at low
cost, by staging shows in unusual venues
and presenting the clothes in experimental
new ways. But irrespective of the approach,
whatever the market level and customer,
the commercial reality is that creativity and
wearability are mutually interdependent if a
fashion business is to succeed.

5   Alexander McQueen's final collection,
    A/W 2010.

INSPIRATION

When developing a collection with a team, the designer or design director will often begin by collating an inspiration board or mood board with tear sheets, artifacts, fabric swatches, travel notes, found pieces, historical and cultural references, fine art, photography, illustrations—anything that represents the initial direction of the overall look or theme for the new collection. Designers will travel the world to collect inspiration, often referencing the cultural dress and local street style in major cities or obscure destinations.

6   Georg Meyer-Wiel used his illustrations of birds and historical costumes as research for his MA final menswear collection.

6

What is a collection?

BLACKBERRY

PEAT

COAL

CRANBERRY

MIDNIGHT

AMBER

BARK

WALNUT

STONE

IVORY

7

7 Poppy Dover, A/W 2013,
color board.

8 Poppy Dover, mood board.

8

Inspiration

9   Edie Campbell, muse to
Hedi Slimane, modeling
his debut collection for
Saint Laurent.

The muse

An ideal or inspirational customer is sometimes known as a *muse* who embodies the designer's style or approach, inputting into the look and promoting the collection and often fragrances too. John Galliano, for example, worked closely with Lady Amanda Harlech, who has since joined Karl Lagerfeld at Chanel. Models, actors, and now celebrities inspire or design their own ranges with the help of a qualified team. Model-of-the-moment and aspiring actress Cara Delevingne with her unique, cool street style is a model and muse for Burberry, appearing on the catwalk and in campaigns for the brand, while also designing and modeling bags for Mulberry.

Hubert de Givenchy was notable for launching the iconic style of the gamine Audrey Hepburn with his designs for the costumes for *Breakfast at Tiffany's*, demonstrating the relationship between the designer as a stylist and the muse. Yves Saint Laurent's muses, an aristocrat, Loulou de la Falaise, and an actress, Catherine Deneuve, were loyal ambassadors throughout his career.

Film

Fashion and film are always linked, and designers will often design costumes for film and theater alongside their fashion collections, as seen recently with Prada designs for *The Great Gatsby*, alongside Brooks Brothers menswear. Armani launched a new soft tailoring look for Richard Gere in *American Gigolo*. Tom Ford directed and designed the clothes for his first film, *A Single Man*, whose protagonist is a fictional muse created by the designer who influenced his menswear collections.

10 Catherine Martin, an Academy Award–winning Costume and Production Designer, in a Miuccia Prada dress, and Baz Luhrmann, who directed, produced, and co-wrote the screenplay for *The Great Gatsby*, attend the *Gatsby* opening on April 30, 2013, in New York City.

DEVELOPMENT

Themes and directions for collections can be enhanced and developed from primary research, regardless of location, time, or season. The research process is an ongoing aspect of the designer's role, and it is unlikely to start from scratch for any one collection.

After discussing shapes and fabrics, the first patterns and toiles will be prepared. These toiles will be recut and refined a number of times in the process from initial idea to final reality. Most designers and manufacturers will hire a model, known as a *fit* or *house* model. This is crucial in refining and confirming exact proportions, detail placement, movement, and overall look. Models are hired specifically for their height and body dimensions, as this information will be crucial to the pattern cutter and also when casting models for a show. Once garments have been bought for retail, they will be resized, with changes made to length, proportion, and so on. This is important if exporting to some international markets, or may simply reflect the type of customer, who may demand a less extreme version of a showpiece.

Depending on the season being developed, additional specialist freelance team members may be contracted to work to specific pieces or looks. These may include knitwear specialists, beading specialists, embroiderers, handcraft tailors, or fashion-print designers. Todd Lynn will commission artwork from illustrators to create his own printed or embroidered fabrics or lace to give something unique to his collections. This collaboration requires a great deal of planning and preparation. As the team grows and the variables within a collection increase, the designer must control this range of activities to ensure that the original vision or brief is still in view. Freelance designers who contribute to the collection may be briefed at the onset or commissioned to produce individual pieces, such as shoes or hats, which will highlight a particular aspect of the collection.

11 The stages involved in the process of developing a collection.

1. Designer > inspiration > visualization > briefing to sample team, including pattern cutter, sample maker and finance (costing and business).

↓

2. Designer > business manager for final costings and ordering for production (materials and manufacturing time).

↓

3. Designer > stylist for final show presentation.

↓

4. Designer > business manager and retail buyers to establish orders and confirm production.

↓

5. Designer > show producer for venue, music, set, ticketing, models, hair and make-up.

↓

6. Designer > business manager and PR to establish press information, future editorial coverage and show; guest lists, which may include VIPs or sponsors.

↓

7. Designer > PR, to cover post-show interviews or requests for editorial coverage. Possible requests for loan garments to be used in photo shoots.

↓

8. Designer > business manager to review orders, confirm production and delivery. Final costings to be agreed.

↓

9. Designer begins to gather information for the next collection or season and plans trade visits to underpin this activity.

Development

12

FABRIC SOURCING

A key part of the designer's role is sourcing fabric. A designer will visit trade fairs twice a year before the start of the following season to source the newest fabrics and view emerging trends. Alternatively, if they have an established relationship with fabric mills, they may develop their own fabrics.

Buying and selling fabric presents a challenge in predicting how much fabric will be required for production of orders—and the possibility of needing to reorder within a season. Too much fabric can result in funds tied up in stock, which then needs to be sold or reused. Too little fabric ordered can result in lost sales and reduced profits. The same consideration must be given to production time—whether it is a small team of machinists or a large-scale factory.

Fabric fairs

Première Vision in Paris, and also now Shanghai, is the most established of the fashion fabric and trend exhibitions. The Indigo section there is known for launching new designers. Messe Frankfurt is one of the world's largest trade fair companies, with twenty textile fairs across nine countries. These include Interstoff, a traditional fabric fair for sourcing silk, wool, and industrially produced and handmade textiles for bulk and ready-to-wear businesses. Also under the Messe Frankfurt umbrella are Texworld, which covers fabric produced in the Far East at a sixth of the cost of European fabrics, offering a cheaper alternative to Première Vision along with Apparelsourcing, Intertextile and Yarn Expo, which show good yarns for knitwear.

Staged twice a year in Florence, Pitti Filati exhibits knitwear graduates and is the main fair for yarns. Linea Pelle in Bologna specifically deals with leather and leather-based products and trends. Smaller fairs include Tissu Lille in France and the Turkish Fabric Fair in London, which welcomes students as well as designers.

At the fairs, designers make appointments to see agents and manufacturers who display their sample ranges, which are delivered to designers in time to plan and develop the new season's ranges. Trend direction information is gathered from the vast range of exhibitors. Most exhibitors at Première Vision are happy to deal with businesses of all sizes for sample orders, but they require a minimum order to ensure production is viable for particular prints, colorways, or fabrics. For smaller orders, manufacturers may levy a surcharge or combine the orders, which delays delivery time. A number of the more established designers will request certain fabrics, prints, or colorways as an exclusive purchase. This additional cost is passed on to the customer and is reflected in the final garment's price.

13 Filmar yarn collection, Pitti Filati, Lucinda Popp.

FORECASTING TRENDS

Existing and emerging fashion trends constantly provide stimulus, and trend information is a key element across all the creative industries. Traditionally, trends have been identified and packaged for designers as forecasting packages, where colors, fabrics, yarns, silhouettes, and graphics are collated into books or presented online and used to predict key looks for the forthcoming season. This detailed trend information may inform or influence a collection in greater depth than a single season's direction or look.

Trend forecasting companies or futurologists will give presentations internally to larger organizations to establish a direction based on the client's needs and aspirations. They employ teams of visual researchers, cool hunters, factual researchers, trend analysts, trend writers, visual editors, and bloggers who focus on social behavior patterns and consumption and reflect on daily life to inform the future.

Trend companies

Trend forecasting includes established international companies Promostyl, Carlin International, Peclers, Nelly Rodi, Trendstop, and Trend Union, and smaller companies, such as The Future Laboratory, Trend Boutique, Studio M, and Mudpie. Carlin will have, for example, fourteen trend books—one for each product area—each presenting macro trends, which are delivered in a visual and tactile book format with fabric and color swatches. Li Edelkoort's forecasting company, Trend Union, produces a collection of trend books and audiovisuals twice a year for the textile and fashion industries. In the UK, The Future Laboratory's website LS:N Global is a trends and insight network that plugs users into what is new, next, and innovative in consumer needs and lifestyle behavior.

As fashion has evolved and information sources are now widely available online, the trend forecasting industry has responded to provide a wider range of products. These include trend intelligence, trend management, international retail trends, customer trends, advertising, catwalk shows, and technology trends, which are all available by subscription. Studio M works closely with clients all over the world to produce bespoke packages for inspiration. They can dip-dye a series of color swatches on base fabrics to create a palette, provide samples of embroidery and specialist trims, and remake elements, such as collars taken from vintage garments, to interpret looks. By offering a full service, clients can then pick and choose elements as required for their own collections.

FORECASTING AGENCY: WGSN

WGSN, the world's leading forecasting agency, provides trend forecasting and analysis to large corporate companies including Marks and Spencer (M&S), Topman, and Puma in the UK, and Tommy Hilfiger and Target in the United States. They anticipate future trends, increase speed to market, make informed decisions, and drive productivity. WGSN demonstrates how key themes apply to forthcoming collections, with trends defined specifically by product for womenswear, menswear, childrenswear, sportswear, and accessories with references to key color silhouettes, styling, and graphics.

LS:N GLOBAL

The lifestyle news network

INSPIRE

SEED   TRENDS ·   INSIGHT ·   INNOVATE   INFORM   INSPIRE ·

My Pinboard
Member Profile

Shop

Home
RSS
Membership Benefits
Contact
The Future Laboratory

Join the Mailing List:

Log out

Announcement:

XX v XY

LS:N GLOBAL
TREND BRIEFING
AUTUMN/ WINTER 2013
OCTOBER 16

DESIGN DIRECTIONS
MACRO / MICRO

DARK ALCHEMY 2013.09.16

Beauty brands are adopting the Black Magic aesthetic and embracing a new gothic direction that blends mediaeval alchemy with emblematic spiritualism.

By Daniela Walker and Victoria Buchanan

Designers are adopting visual cues that are evocative of our Black Magic design direction that we identified in 2012 in beauty packaging and retail spaces as consumers look for products that offer an antidote to the chaos of 21st-century living.

To match the dour mood of this recessionary era, products are becoming similarly austere with a nod to alchemy and symbolism. This trend towards a kind of visual mysticism that hints at something sinister reflects an overall mood for 2013/2014,' says Bella Blissett, beauty columnist for The Mail on Sunday's You magazine. 'A new take on beauty has emerged: Darker Moodier. This is a woman who is slightly unhinged,' she adds. Referencing a pre-technological era, when magic was real and science was its own form of magic, the packaging is bewitching, mystical and unexplainable.

French perfume brand Les Liquides Imaginaires' identity is represented by an enigmatic talisman that is derived from symbols of Christianity, Kabbelah, Islam and Paganism. Its candles come in black triangular boxes stamped with the emblem and nothing more. The limited-edition fragrances have Latin names – Sancti, Fortis and Tumultu – reminiscent of incantations and potions. The brand is available at its bespoke perfumery, where bottles are displayed with labels facing outwards behind a counter, as if it were a 19th-century apothecary.

HERBIVORE BOTANICALS

BAMBOO CHARCOAL

tea tree · lavender

In the same vein, Herbivore Botanicals' minimalist black and white packaging has an instantly recognisable emblem, the triangle, at the heart of its graphic identity. Triangles are shrouded in mysticism, prevalent in masonic societies and alchemy. The packaging reflects the organic product, calling back to a time when people turned to nature for remedies.

'We strive to bring product and packaging together to make a line that is unique with a minimalist simplicity,' the designers tell LS:N Global. It is similar to a forerunner of the Sort of Coal aesthetic, which uses the dark, mysterious nature of its product combined with pared-down packaging to draw in consumers.

Belgian designer Nico Uytterhaegen's Nonsincense fragrances come in black lacquered bottles made from molten rubber, which is scraped and dripped by hand. Conjuring up images of Western esotericism, Uytterhaegen's line was inspired by alchemists' perfume-making, mixing together a few ingredients such as vetiver, patchouli and ylang-ylang. The objective was to create a mysterious and old object that is different from the pure beauty in the cosmetics industry,' says the designer. 'We try to create beauty aggressively and sensitively.'

Taking on Revivalist thinking and a nostalgia for old-world mysticism, brands are adopting a minimalist, apothecary-style aesthetic. Embrace magical thinking, do away with traditional notions of what beauty means and be darker.

06
GLAZED SKIN
FOUNDATION CREAM

⊕ More Like This

14

15

15 Compiling a mood board at
The Future Laboratory.

14 **The Future Laboratory macro
trends on LS:N Global.**

Forecasting trends

Archiving is now common across all levels of the fashion market, where discarded ideas or prototypes can be revisited and reconsidered for future collections. Source pieces can include items from a designer's own archive of past collections. These pieces may form part of a new collection, as replicas cut in different fabrics or prints, for example, or may instead influence fresh development. Sometimes a collection can be created using "rails" or "grids," where images, garments, and fabrics are collated into a three-dimensional collage that captures a theme or design direction, illustrating the color, shapes, and details involved to create a cohesive look. This is useful for all team members involved in the development and realization processes, and it helps to inform decision making. It is important to note that the processes involved are evolutionary and changes, additions, and deletions will occur throughout the development time frame. Research and development activities are interactive and often dictate even last-minute revisions and changes, but the designer or design director will have the overall and final decision on the complete collection content and look.

Photographic archiving is used to record the development of draped toiles on stands, as staged versions of an idea, or images of the collection in individual outfits or looks. The latter is useful when allocating outfits to individual models and planning the running order for a fashion show. Many designers use photography to compile images for possible research, and because much of the collection's development is visually based, this saves time and establishes a common visual language. Photography plays an enormous part in the documentation, development, and archiving of fashion garments. With the accessibility of digital photography and wireless technology, it is now possible for designers to source and collate an endless number of images for personal reference databases.

16 **A series of boards by Holly Berry, showing photographic archiving.**

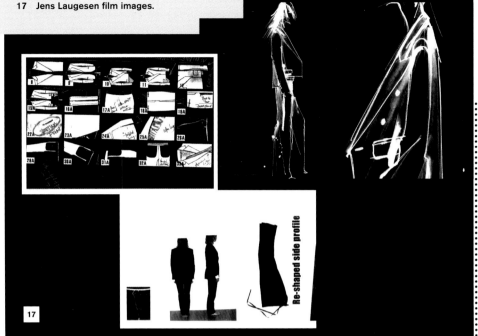

17

Re-shaped side profile

EDITING COLLECTIONS

Regardless of how or when a designer begins a new collection, there will inevitably be problems that challenge the most careful planning. Deliveries, mistakes, and delays are variables that must be expected and managed. Additional problems can occur when the designer subcontracts or employs freelance specialists to collaborate on the collection and the final show.

Even when most pieces are complete, fitted, and photographed as outfits or looks, further changes may be required if the whole collection is adrift of the original vision, or the range is imbalanced in color, garment type, or fabric. During the development cycle, it is very common for ideas to be rejected, for new aspects to be introduced to the collection plan, and for nearly everything to run late. Although this is the popular view of the creative process involved within the fashion industry, it accurately acknowledges the complexity and convergent energies involved.

Editorial decisions are based on the whole collection working as envisaged at the outset. The designer may acknowledge that some pieces or outfits have not worked as well as hoped, or may perhaps look repetitive. Changes or rejections exist as part of the development process and are common at every market level.

USEFUL ARCHIVE SOURCES

Wayne Hemingway set up an online archive for the Land of Lost Content museum www.lolc.org.uk.

This huge collection of popular British culture images is a useful resource for students and industry alike.

Editing collections

THE TEAM

The development process is cyclical and depends on a number of team members performing specialist activities. The core in-house team at a designer label will usually consist of the designer, a pattern cutter, and a sample machinist, with interns taken on to cut out samples, source trims, and perform general duties.

As the number of collections being developed increases, so too will the number of staff on the team or in the business. Many larger companies (designer and retail) establish separate business units or divisions to cater to the business demands and development processes involved. As such, within the largest fashion businesses, it is possible to have senior design positions with the responsibility for a very specific product area, such as men's casual knitwear or women's jersey separates.

Designer

The designer is the central member of the team. Whether at an haute couture house in Paris or an online multi-brand company, he or she is ultimately responsible for creating the collection—from the initial inspiration and design stages to overseeing first samples for selling. The designer will brief a team of assistants or the studio staff to create further research or feedback from development.

The designer's role can vary according to the size of the company; however, all designers must have the ability to make a decision and follow it through to create a desirable end product. In a large team, a designer will begin with designing for one area or product type, for example, formal dresses or casual tops.

As the designer progresses through the company, he or she may ultimately become the design director responsible for all product areas and the overall design vision for the season. Within a medium-size company the designer may be responsible for a range or label within the brand and may cover more than one area. In a small company the designer will design the entire collection with the help of assistants to produce first samples.

Designers will inevitably have multiple working relations, including dealing with fabric and trim merchants, yarn suppliers and textile designers, buyers and merchandisers, costing clerks and accountants, and PR agents and stylists. The designer will take the responsibility for all decision making and amendments throughout the design process. The ability to communicate is just as important as being creative; in fact, it is often key to success.

18 April 7, 1965: Yves Saint Laurent, former wonder boy of Dior, working at his own fashion house in Paris.

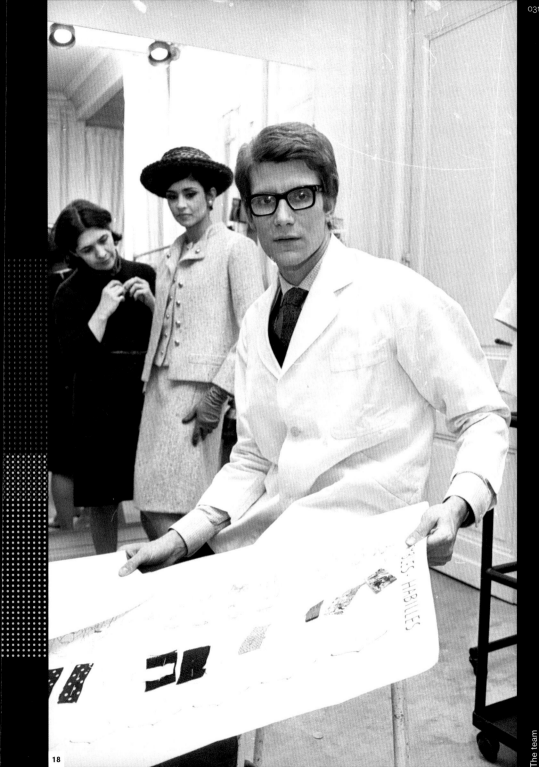

The team

19 E. Tautz students—working on embroidery.

20 E. Tautz yarns—color.

Pattern cutter

The pattern cutter will work with the designer's images and drawings, which convey the direction and look of the collection. Often working with the designer and sample machinist, the pattern cutter's responsibility is to help realize an idea or vision in three dimensions.

Working predominantly with the overall silhouette sketched by the designer, the pattern cutter's skill is to interpret the shape and proportion for the new collection and to adapt existing block patterns or produce new patterns from scratch depending on the designer's vision. Creative pattern cutters will have bespoke skills that are sympathetic to the designer's signature style and will be able to use appropriate cloth to achieve the overall silhouette. Pattern cutters are also employed to work on less creative pieces, such as adapting previous patterns and grading samples. Nowadays graded patterns are produced digitally; however, the cutter needs to be familiar with the principles of grading a pattern according to different body shapes and sizes.

Pattern cutters will produce a first sample in calico or cheap cotton fabric called a *toile*, which is then fitted on an in-house fit model or agency model. They may specialize in draping or modeling on the stand or in flat pattern cutting, or a combination of both. Pattern cutters are often freelance and brought in to work on specific collections or to oversee the sampling process in factories to ensure the fit of the garment is to the designer's specifications.

THE BLOCKS

Designers will usually compile a series of blocks from which styles can be developed. A block is a basic pattern shape covering the upper body or the lower body, such as a shirt or a skirt. Each designer's blocks are refined basic shapes, often unique, and the result of painstaking measurements, fittings, and placement of darts and seam lines. Blocks are often closely guarded secrets; they form the basis for excellent cut and fit when modified. Toiles derived from previous collections may be included for future reference, and designers can also unpick sourced garments to study cut and construction techniques. This practice is used within companies across all market levels.

21 E. Tautz students—from the Royal School of Needlework (RSN).

Sample cutter

Some studios employ sample cutters who work at great speed and accuracy to cut out the first sample patterns in the correct fabric for the sample machinist to make up. Smaller companies will expect the pattern cutters to perform this task; sometimes sample cutting is part of the process given to student interns gaining work experience. Sample cutters are also responsible for cutting out lays, which are layers of fabric with the patterns laid on top and cut with a band knife or rotary cutter to produce multiple samples. Larger companies usually computerize this process, allowing samples to be cut out in factories based overseas.

Sample machinist

The sample machinist is different from a production machinist on a factory production line as they are skilled at interpreting and sewing samples from a designer's sketch. Designers will sketch a shape with a suggestion of detail with fabric attached that often has to be realized by the pattern cutter and sample machinist. Sample machinists need to be adaptable and enjoy working on new designs; however, they will be skilled in a certain area and fabric or skin (e.g., chiffon or leather), which is why ideally there will be different sample machinists for different collections.

This process is far easier when the designer, pattern cutter, and sample machinist are based in the same building; however, first samples are often made in factories overseas. Sample machinists work closely with the pattern cutter to make up the toiles and first samples cut in cloth. The toile is made first; it is a replica for shape but will not be finished with overlocking or any detailing. Details, such as buttonholes and pockets, will be drawn onto the calico and sampled for finish. Once the initial toiles are assembled, the designer and pattern cutter will adjust the size and position of collars and pockets and alter hem lengths before cutting the sample in the final cloth. In larger companies, a sample-room manager will ensure that deadlines are met across a wide range of sampling requirements. Machinists will be given bundles of cut work and a designer's annotated sketch or a full specification sheet that contains a drawing, accurate measurements, fitting details, a detailed technical drawing, and fabric and trims specification.

Studio manager

In a company that employs a team of designers and pattern cutters, a studio manager coordinates all the functions between the sampling and production processes. This is especially important if the company works from multiple sites.

The team

Product developer

Not every company will have a product developer, but within larger companies and especially sports brands that have various products within their ranges, the product developer will be responsible for innovation of product type and new technologies in fabric and construction. Product developers will work closely with design directors and marketing managers to identify gaps in the market and pilot new products that enhance the company's current range by introducing loss leaders to gain market share in a competitive environment. Product developers may have a product design background with an interest in fashion or may be a fashion graduate with an interest in product design.

All garments within a collection that are produced to sell must be costed. This is either the responsibility of the designer or, in larger companies, a costing administrator. Costings are based on two main components: materials (direct cost) and labor (indirect cost). They are a key part of technical packs, which include detailed specification sheets of sketches, measurements, fabric and trim references, and special instructions for finishes.

The costing process links sampling and production and ensures that the designer's vision is carried through to the shop floor. Samples are reworked and sometimes fabrics are substituted if the cost is too high after margins are added (margins can be up to 250 percent for some stores to cover their costs). More and more, samples are being sent to factories in the Far East to be copied at a far cheaper rate for both fabric and labor. But with the current and increasing emphasis on sustainable and organic fabrics, costs are also rising, so marketing plays an important part in promoting the added value and social conscience.

Buyers and merchandisers

Fashion buyers are judged by sales and departmental profitability. As such, most buyers are keen to investigate new lines or designers capable of adding to an established retail business. Quality, reliability of delivery, and reordering are essential considerations in addition to cost. The relationship between designers and buyers is important and can launch a successful career; Joan Burstein at Browns in London, for example, bought John Galliano's graduation collection and featured it in the store's windows.

In large companies the role of the merchandiser is equal to that of the designer; they often work together to create and edit the collection to a price. Merchandisers are responsible for the pieces of a collection that end up in stores. They are accountants and decision makers with a creative understanding for the product. In the United States the merchandiser is the designer's counterpart. In the UK, however, merchandisers deal with figures and quantities, working alongside the buyers, who are responsible for ranging and selecting from the directive of the design team. Working to budgets, the designer, merchandiser, and buyer are all responsible for a company's commercial success.

Stylists and PR agents

Designers and producers will work with a fashion stylist when considering the presentation of the collection for press, buyers, or the consumer. Usually working on a freelance basis, the stylist will oversee each element of the collection to ensure that the original vision is realized. The stylist may also be the main contact person for coordinating a catwalk show. They can work with casting directors to select models that suit the collection and offer advice on hair and makeup, footwear, and accessories, as well as the music used for the show.

Experienced stylists work closely with the designer from concept to final looks. Often part of the original team as a muse or facilitator, the stylist can transform even the most basic fashion piece into a key look or trend before it is shown to the public.

PR agents represent the designer outside the company and promote the collection to secure preshow press and follow-up press, including on blogs. They can also work in a stylist's capacity, being responsible for the look of the catwalk show and working with photographers to create editorial content and advertising for magazines. PR agents also distribute lookbooks and arrange appointments with buyers.

Resources

A typical start-up designer business may well be located in small or adapted premises. The basic requirements, if samples are to be made in the design studio, are a cutting table, industrial machines, and pressing equipment. There should be allocated space for storage of fabrics (current season sampling fabric and production fabric), trims, pattern paper, final patterns, and hanging equipment. A space for meetings and a showroom for visitors are desirable for a professional appearance. Most rental spaces for fashion companies will be configured to allow for all these functions. Depending on how a collection is produced, it is common to outsource most activities to specialist providers, such as pattern cutters and sample makers. This relies on subcontractors or "cut, make, and trim" outworker units being able to understand the designer's requirements and specifications.

Regardless of the exact provision of resources, overheads and costs must be carefully managed and built into the garment costings. Many designers starting out with a new fashion label fail due to inadequate knowledge of the business side. Some of the most successful designers, such as Yves Saint Laurent, Giorgio Armani, and UK designer Betty Jackson founded their businesses with a business or financial expert—thereby allowing clear role definitions within the company.

22 Katie Grand, Giles Deacon.

The team

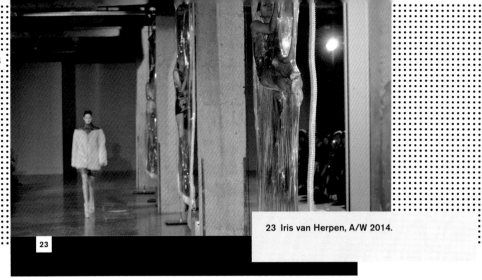

23 Iris van Herpen, A/W 2014.

23

SHOWING THE COLLECTION

Most designer collections are shown internationally as part of a seasonal show schedule of Spring/Summer and Autumn/Winter. This traditional method of showing the latest looks is the same in every fashion capital, with a week-long schedule of fashion shows attracting buyers and press. Major fashion houses rely on these shows to promote their brand and will more often sell through a smaller salon show or exhibition to targeted clients or through pre-collections aimed specifically at loyal customers. But increasingly designers are choosing to show their work in alternative ways, either through an exhibition, installation, or online presentation. Nick Knight's broadcasting website (www.showstudio.com) showcased Shelley Fox's early installations. The website continues to promote alternative ways of showing collections. He promotes the work of Gareth Pugh and Aitor Thorp, showing films of their installations instead of traditional catwalk shows. Some designers' collections are based on fashion as fine-art pieces or collaborations with artists. These garments may be influential to fashion designers but are rarely seen as fashion pieces because they are not intended to be worn as clothing, but rather they serve to broaden our perceptions of clothes.

For example, in the 1930s, Elsa Schiaparelli collaborated with Surrealist artist Salvador Dali to create playful trompe l'oeil prints and accessories. This collaboration was intellectually interesting, highly influential, and is still referenced today. Fashion designer and artist Lucy Orta (www.studio-orta.com) uses garments as a narrative element within a series of internationally acclaimed exhibitions. There is no immediate fashion application to these images, yet the influence of this work can inform the fashion process and consumer.

Another example of fashion collections showcased for enjoyment, rather than immediate commercial application, is the curated exhibition, such as "Superheroes: Fashion and Fantasy" at the Metropolitan Museum of Art in New York, a thematically curated exhibition of fashion pieces based on comic-book characters and their style. In addition, retrospective exhibitions, designed to celebrate a designer's career, may create a fresh interest in a particular style or look. Examples include Giorgio Armani, Viktor & Rolf, and Bill Gibb.

24 Shelley Fox's "Philadelphia Florist"
exhibition at the Stanley Picker Gallery,
Kingston University.

Showing the collection

CAPSULE COLLECTIONS

Some designers offer an additional, smaller collection in December/January, known as the cruise collection (or holiday collection in the United States). These collections are primarily summer lines, prepared and available before the new spring ranges are fully delivered into stores. Cruise collections are popular with wealthy customers who holiday at this time of year. Increasingly clients want exclusivity. Designers such as Nicolas Ghesquière at Balenciaga have reintroduced specialist capsule collections. Similar to haute couture, these collections are shown to private customers and are not available to a wider audience.

Lookbooks

Though often spectacular, fashion shows may not be necessary for commercial success. Although the catwalk shows are attended by buyers and press, the pieces bought for retail may be significantly different (i.e., more wearable) and are selected before the season's collection is shown. Designers and retailers compile each collection into a lookbook, where each piece is ranged as looks and photographed as such. Away from the catwalk, decisions are made on what the customer will want when the items are available. This buying or selection process may take place on the designer's premises or else in a rented studio. Designers who show in London, for example, may be invited to sell at events such as Trenois or Rendez-Vous in Paris. They can rent a salon for the duration of the selling period—usually up to two weeks—so that buyers can make appointments to see the collection.

25

25 A look book example from Satyenkumar Patel's A/W 2012 collection.

Catwalk shows

Catwalk presentations are a way of showing collections in an experiential, idealized context in order to create press coverage as well as orders. Costs and workload increase dramatically and at times may create no orders for the collection. However, many designers secure financial support or backing for their catwalk shows, which are seen as essential to building a designer's business or brand.

All fashion shows follow a similar process in production, the variables being budget and scale. The budget must allow for venue, models, music, hair, makeup, show producer, ticketing, and promotion. Costs tend to be high and planning is exhaustive, as shows are typically "live" and scrutinized by the press, buyers, and fashion experts. Decisions have to be made on each aspect of the production and invariably there are problems that demand patience and flexibility. At this stage of the process, deadlines become critical, as the show will be scheduled for an exact time and date and rehearsals are required to ensure that the models have time to change and also understand any choreography requirements.

The collection will usually be shown as looks, or exits, where each piece is coordinated to present the designer's vision. Larger collections will be shown by color, fabric, or occasion. Shows usually last about half an hour, depending on the number of looks or exits.

26

26 Louis Vuitton, S/S 2014.

28

27, 28 Louis Vuitton, S/S 2014.

MARTIN RAYMOND,
Cofounder of The Future Laboratory and Chief Editor of LS:N Global

What did you study and where?
I did an MA in Fashion Journalism at CSM [Central Saint Martins] after a background in journalism in Dublin. Following my MA, I worked as a freelancer for *Creative Review*, *Elle* magazine, and then became the editor of *Fashion Weekly*.

I was also a presenter on a TV program about fashion in Dublin called *Head to Toe*. I then worked for Maggie Norden teaching BA Fashion Journalism at LCF [London College of Fashion]. From 1997 to 2001, I was the editor of *Viewpoint* for David Shah who also published *Textile View* and *View on Colour* with Li Edelkoort.

How did you start the company?
Readers used *Viewpoint* to ask strategic questions about client need rather than trend, which led me to establish The Future Laboratory consultancy in 2001 with my partner Chris Sanderson as the Creative Director.

Why did you set up your website "LS:N Global"?
To capture consumers' insight into lifestyle. We have a section called "Future Poll," which provides quantitative analysis on markets. LS:N will look at inspiration and design direction and aesthetic material alongside the behavioral aspect of a trend to provide an online context.

How many do you have in your team?
We have fifty-eight full-time people in our team, including myself and Chris Sanderson, the other Cofounder of the company. We employ 50 percent male and 50 percent female and recruit teams by ages to represent all age groups. We structure our teams really carefully into three areas: visual researchers, factual researchers, what's new and next?

Within these teams we employ trend analysts, trend writers, visual and inside editors. Trend analysts take anomalies, look at patterns, and spread globally synthesizing trends. Trend writers look at evidence and put together the bigger thesis. From this dossier they come up with a proposition for macro trends.

What is a collection?

Micro trends are ideas fermenting, which will evolve into macro trends or are derivative of them. The team will then engage in cultural triangulation made up of observation, interrogation, and intuition to make decisions on forecasting.

How do you start trend research?
We look at what is happening globally and put this into a context to understand lifestyle sectors. We will look for common themes or trends and the anomalies within the patterns (i.e., organic, authentic, bespoke will be mapped with science, biotech, or magic).

The consumer is concerned about things in life that will elevate intangible emotional experiences. Luxury is no longer five-star hotels but sleeping out on an ice cap, which will be double the cost. Large companies are looking at behavioral shifts and how this relates to brand acquisition. Drivers behind the trends are mapped and evidenced to forecast for the economic market. Expectations are different, which needs to be reflected in the brand's value.

Who are your clients?
We have fourteen different sections to our business, including fashion, which amounts to a third of our business; retail; luxury; interiors; technology; hospitality; travel; food; and financial services. We focus on the strategic rather than specific for global clients, which include LMVH, Gucci, Chanel, H&M, Selfridges, Harrods, M&S, Condé Nast, Estée Lauder, L'Oréal, British Airways, AMEX [American Express], HSBC, Nationwide, Absolut Vodka, and Jameson Whiskey.

How do you influence designers' collections?
Brand teams work on strategic development to establish the tone of voice and how the customers engage online. Marketing teams then follow brand requirements rather than the traditional buying teams.

29 **The Future Laboratory.**

Interview: Martin Raymond

Interview

SHELLEY FOX,
Fashion and Textiles Designer

How do you start your collections?

My collections don't start with a blank sheet of paper. With "Philadelphia Florist," I found three diaries in a flea market and lived with them for three years; then, when a fellowship came up at the Stanley Picker Gallery at Kingston University, I thought the diaries could be used for the project. I am constantly collecting things but I don't always know when and where I am going to use them. I never dump an idea once the collection is done, as ideas will go somewhere else in the future. I think there is a constant thread of interest weaving its way through each collection, with a different point of view depending on how you are feeling at the time. In 1998 I produced my first installation, called the "Braille" collection, which became an iconic collection in the Joseph store during London Fashion Week. It has since been shown in a number of international exhibitions; most recently in the exhibition called "Archaeology of the Future" by forecasting guru Li Edelkoort, in Paris and Eindhoven.

How many collections do you design a year?

Now that I am located in New York, and working around my professorship at Parson's, I could only manage one project a year or over a longer period. I think it is still important for me to develop my own way of working.

I stopped producing collections to sell in 2004. The next big project after that was "Fashion at Belsay," an installation that was staged in a nineteenth-century house in Northumbria, England. It was based around clothing but as packed walls rather than mannequin displays.

Do you compile a color palette and, if so, how?

I am not an overly colorful collection designer as I tend to focus more on silhouette and texture, but there have been collections where I have worked with scorched yellow wools, Morse-code-printed fabrics, and burnt sequin fabrics. Color is not a priority at the beginning of a collection. The all-white "Philadelphia Florist" collection came about from a white fabric I sourced from a company in Japan; it was more about fabric manipulation than print.

How and where do you source fabrics?

A combination of Première Vision for good basics, such as great suitings, and shirtings from the UK. I have developed an identity for making my own fabrics, such as felting from my graduation collection, using yarn supplied by John Smedley, knitted at Nottingham Trent and felted in washing machines.

For production I train assistants in the felting process to know the right handle. No two garments are the same in production and the beauty is in the uniqueness.

What is a collection?

30

30 "Negative" Collection 2006: The collection was supported by the Arts Council of England and was first launched at the Victoria and Albert Museum as part of the "Spectres" exhibition curated by Judith Clark.

cutting. Once the fit is right on the stand, the shapes are then made into a flat pattern.

How do you create your first samples, and how many are made for each collection?

First samples are made in the studio, but the knitwear goes out to be sampled in the factories straight from spec sheets, which have already been sampled in toile form in the studio. For my own label, agents used to select samples from Japan that were relevant to them and they were remade.

How many looks on average per collection are for catwalk only?

I made twelve outfits for my Masters degree collection at Central Saint Martins, but I have done up to forty-five outfits, which can cost too much money to repeat in different colors and fabrics for production. The collections were often confusing when they got too big. I keep the best press pieces and usually a copy of each piece for archive and sell the rest through sample sales.

Do you commission textiles, such as knit, print, weave, and embroidery?

I have worked with Knitwear Designer Tomoko at Livingstone Studios for chunky hand-knits when she was still at the Royal College of Art. She worked on a couple of collections for me. I also worked closely with Todd and Duncan who sponsored yarns for three seasons and then the clothing was produced in a factory in Hawick, Scotland.

Do you have any second lines to the main range?

No, as I never really designed the collections that way. It was more important for me to focus on the main collection.

How do you develop your shapes and silhouettes: flat pattern, draping, or modeling on the stand?

The early circle cutting was based on cutting up crude drawings to create new silhouettes. It was a process that developed over some early collections; it was influenced by my partner, who is a fine artist and has a different head on my work. Shapes are also developed on the stand and then photographs [are] taken of the details; the design is developed back and forth between drawing and photography and eventually we work on the

How do you work with stylists and PR for selling the collection?

I have worked with different stylists in the past, such as Nancy Rhode and, more recently, Jane Howard for the "Spectres" show at the V&A [Victoria and Albert]. I also worked with Abnormal PR—they held each collection for six months to show to press and worked with me closely on the shows.

Interview: Shelley Fox

HOLLY FULTON,
Fashion-Print Designer

travels. I have a large collection of books and am quite a hoarder. I often pick up things that might not be obvious sources of inspiration but can lead me on to different trains of thought. Once I have an idea, then I'll start looking into it with greater depth and often a muse or leading lady will pop up who forms the basis of my woman for the season. I use the Internet a lot and also my collection of books and magazines, film, and music help enhance the threads of ideas once they begin, too.

Where did you study?
I did my degree in Fashion at Edinburgh College of Art, followed by a postgraduate diploma in Fashion at the same institute, and finally an MA in Womenswear at the Royal College of Art.

What did you do when you graduated?
I went directly to work for Lanvin in Paris on their embellished womenswear and accessories and returned to the UK and began my own label in 2009.

How did you set up your own label?
I was asked to take part in Fashion East, a London-based initiative where three new designers showcase their work in a joint show. I showed my AW09 collection there, and my business formed from there.

How do you research your collections?
Collection research can stem from numerous sources and is often led by a place I have visited or objects I have come across on my

How many collections do you design a year?
I currently design two main line collections a year and focus other time on collaborative projects.

How do you compile your color palette?
Color palette will be dictated by research and the early direction of the collection; we have signature color combinations that we often feature, generally anything which enhances a strong graphic and creates a pop statement. I tend to go for quite different color stories each season and break the collection down into color related blocks for the show.

How do you source your base cloths?
As we work mainly with print, the majority of our bases are those which are recommended through our printers who can guarantee how the base will react to print and behave as a

What is a collection?

fabrication. Often we will be looking for unusual fabrications to enhance and compliment the print and embellishment within the range—I enjoy pushing the conceived notions of what fabrics can be paired and bringing something different into the arena of contemporary fashion. My ethos is to use contemporary materials and techniques but rework them with a high-end attention to detail.

How do you design your prints?

The key prints in the collection start off from hand-rendered drawings I do, which we then take and play with digitally. Things often change significantly during the run up to the show, and ideas can only really evolve once you see the color representation of the print when it arrives. My work is very geared around color, and it is crucial it is conveyed onto the fabric surface correctly. I love brights, and quite jarring combinations excite me. The print often takes shape quite naturally during the design process; there is a lot of snap decision making along the way, and that's really what keeps the creative juices flowing.

How do you develop your silhouettes?

I usually work with what look like fairly simplistic silhouettes, as they allow the maximum area for surface pattern, which is the mainstay of my work. I will try to have repeat styles within each collection, to allow for continuity, and strengthen the ideas behind the range, often diffusing the more elaborate version down into something more accessible for stores. I like large, clean shapes and also engineered patterns—recently we have been including shapes, which appear in the jewelry and accessories, as panels into garments to create cohesive and strong ranges and carve out a distinctive identity for the label.

Do you work with a pattern cutter?

Yes, I have freelance cutters who come in mid-season to help me develop the range and both my studio manager and assistant can cut.

Where do you create your first samples?

We undertake all of the toiling process in-house and make the show samples with selected manufacturers or in-house.

Where do you manufacture your collection for production?

We conduct most of our manufacturing in the UK, with the exception of the embellishment and print, which we do abroad. All garments are made up in the UK, either through factories or in-house machinists.

How do you present your collection to clients?

I showcase my work at a show during London Fashion Week, then participate in static showrooms in London and Paris for sales. We often tour the collection to Los Angeles and New York for British Fashion Council sponsored showrooms and are open to undertaking private appointments for stores and clients.

Who do you work with for selling the collection?

We take part in British Fashion Council sponsored showrooms in Paris for sales, where an in-house team handles the sales, and I will generally be present throughout to liaise with stores and press.

Do you collaborate with other companies under your own label?

Absolutely, it is a fundamental part of running a successful label these days as it allows you to broaden your customer reach and target new audiences while generating essential revenue and media round the label.

Interview: Holly Fulton

TODD LYNN,
Fashion Designer

Where did you study?

At Ryerson University in Toronto, Canada, for BA Fashion, and CSM for MA Fashion.

What happened after you left the MA course?

I worked for Roland Mouret and did bespoke work for musicians Marilyn Manson, U2, and The Rolling Stones. Since then I have made pieces for Beyoncé, Janet Jackson, Rihanna, and [the] Black Eyed Peas.

How and when did you start your own label?

I left Roland Mouret and took a gamble and set up my own label, which was self-financed from bespoke work for musicians. This was in 2006, and I presented my first collection in September of that year.

What and who inspires you?

I am always inspired by art and film both current and historical. In fashion I am inspired by designers who are able to cut—designers like Yves Saint Laurent, Claude Montana, and Alexander McQueen.

What is a collection?

How do you research your collections?

I start with the world at large in the news, the environment, economically, and emotionally. Fashion represents a moment in time. My concept needs to say something about the time we live in. Currently, I am researching deconstruction. Everything from Jacques Derrida (the French philosopher who coined the phrase) right through to designers (both fashion and architectural) who first experimented with the concept. I like taking a complicated idea and simplifying it for a show or presentation.

I read books on philosophy, art, history, and source out-of-print books and exhibition catalogs found from book resellers online.

Where do you source your fabrics?

I go to fabric trade shows like PV, as well as visiting mills and tanneries directly to develop exclusive fabrics (i.e., jacquards and prints).

How many collections do you produce in a year?

Two womenswear collections, often with two menswear collections shown within the womenswear presentation.

How many looks do you have in your collection?

I will make around fifty unique pieces and show approximately thirty total looks as separates. There are usually fifteen fabric

31

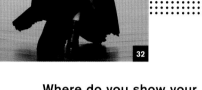

31 Todd Lynn,
A/W 2013, Look 1.

32 Todd Lynn,
A/W 2013, Look 2.

32

groups, which are done in two or three colorways.

Where do you make your samples?
I produce samples in factories in Europe and produce showpieces in ateliers and my studio in [the] UK.

Who do you collaborate with?
Shaun Leane for jewelry and metal showpieces, Sid Bryan of Sibling for knitwear, Graphic Designer Marcus James for prints and graphic elements in fabrics, and Christian Louboutin for shoes.

What do you think the difference is between a collection and a range?
A collection is a creative statement, a vibe rather than exact pieces, more a signature look, whereas a range is about a product commercially driven by the customer needs through a range plan.

What is your signature look?
Razor-sharp tailoring playing close to the gender confusion line but not making women look masculine.

Where do you show your collections?
London Fashion Week catwalk on schedule.

How do you sell your collections?
In a showroom in Paris.

Who are your clients?
Detail (Seoul), Dover Street Market, Havana (Dublin), L'Inde le Palais (Bologna), L'Eclaireur (Paris), Marais (Melbourne), Maxfield (Los Angeles), Net-a-Porter.com, Sanahunt (Kiev), Sauvage (Almaty), The Wall (Tokyo).

Where do you produce your collections?
Everything is made in Europe (UK, France, Italy).

Do you do any design consultancy?
Yes, Debenhams/Edition new diffusion collection alongside Jonathan Saunders, Marios Schwab, Preen, and E. Tautz, as well as collaborations with Topshop and John Lewis and Linda Farrow—sunglasses.

Interview: Todd Lynn

Interview

RICHARD NICOLL,
Fashion Designer

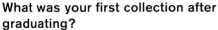

What was your first collection after graduating?

After freelancing for other companies (Topshop, Matthew Williamson, and Bora Aksu) and assisting stylists, Mandi Lennard PR asked me to do a small capsule collection of eight dresses for Autumn/Winter '04 called "Twisted." This was developed from my graduate collection, which was sporty with engineered paneling based on couture techniques. Lulu Kennedy at Fashion East saw it and sponsored the winter version, which included jackets. I met my business partner who turned my Spring/Summer '06 collection into a reality and sold it to b store in London. I did three "New Generation" shows, which were unprecedented; one of them was a slide show, which was a collaboration with a stylist.

How do you start your collections?

I start with silhouette, then research, which starts with mood then color palette. I produce a basic toile that informs a few outfits. I design the components separately, such as five ideas for five bottoms, then sleeves separately, so that pieces build up. I then draw the outfits in line-ups.

How many collections do you design?

I design two collections twice a year and two pre-collections.

How many are in your team?

There are four cutters, one for tailoring, and I work with Jacob, who is a stylist.

How and where do you source fabrics?

I source fabrics from stock that mills carry and also agents, such as an Italian agent that carries specialist silks from Tessio, and I use fabrics from Canepa in Switzerland for shirtings.

Where do you produce your samples?

I have them made in factories in Poland and France for tailoring and dresses; shirts are made in England.

How many pieces on average per collection are for catwalk only?

About 10 to 15 percent are for catwalk only and are couture pieces.

How many pieces/exits are in each collection and does this vary by season or line?

It can be anything from twenty-three outfits to thirty-nine (which was the last collection and too many); usually about thirty-five for the main collection, with fewer in a pre-collection.

How many second lines to the main range do you have?

I design a range for Thomas Pink, which started out with shirts and has now moved

33 Richard Nicoll, A/W 2013.

into dresses (I have done a photo shoot using model Ben Grimes, which is very different for them). I also design a range for Designer Collaborations at Topshop. I also do a shirt range called Richard Nicoll Shirt for Barneys in New York.

Do you collaborate with other sponsors or brands?

I work with Christian Louboutin on shoes, Serapian for bags, and Ksubi for sunglasses. I do the entire look with the running order, including accessories. My hats for the collections are made by Jeffrey Pullman.

34 Richard Nicoll, A/W 2013.

Interview: Richard Nicoll

Interview

FELIPE ROJAS LLANOS,
Designer

Where did you study?

I studied at Central Saint Martins.

What did you do when you graduated?

I loved the two graduate collections I did: "The Little Prince Goes to the Opera" and "Suspended Animation." I had worked very hard to create a signature with these two collections. Once I had done them, I decided to create a new menswear collection and set up my label under my name, I applied to MAN [a collaboration between Topman and Fashion East] and showed the following London Fashion Week and have been working on creating collections since then.

How did you set up your own label?

I set it up my label with a partner, so we divided the workload. I am not good with paperwork, so I focused mostly on the designing and the feel of the collection. Setting up a label is a learning curve that every season comes with new challenges, commitments, and responsibilities.

How do you research your collections?

I spend a lot of time on research every season. I don't really have a method of working since inspiration for me has always come from various sources every season. I mainly research films and graphic novels to create a mood or a story that always centers the collection.

How many collections do you design a year?

I have been making two collections a year, but from next year, I am starting a unisex womenswear collection as well.

How do you compile your color palette?

The palette always starts with an inspiring still from a film, such as Michael Powell and Emeric Pressburger's *The Red Shoes* when the protagonist, Victoria, is walking up that long staircase in her emerald cape, dress and red hair contrasting her outfit, or the tone of the Elizabeth Taylor film *Butterfield 8*. From there I gather samples to create the mood via colors; the color palette is vital to the outcome of the collection.

How do you source your base cloths?

I spend a large amount of time gathering and comparing different cloth samples. I get it from various agents, mainly from Italy and Japan. It is very important that the cloth moves a certain way for my designs to get that "come to life" feel.

How do you design your prints?

I don't design prints for my collections, it's more about the color palette. Saying that,

What is a collection?

35 Felipe Rojas Llanos,
A/W 2010.

35

I have drawn a couple of prints for other projects, but it's mostly loose hand-drawn sketches or characters I have made up.

How do you develop your silhouettes?

I started developing my silhouette when I created my BA collection titled "The Little Prince Goes to the Opera." The shapes were inspired from '50s womenswear couture shapes. Cristóbal Balenciaga mainly inspired my graduate collection, the shapes are all created with the idea of transforming a womenswear shape into menswear one, a lot of thought and time go into creating interesting shapes that are as seamless as possible.

Do you work with a pattern cutter?

I work with a creative pattern cutter that I met during my studies at Central Saint Martins. I have been lucky to meet really talented people along the way. I used to work with another pattern cutter that moved away to Australia, a great pattern cutter is incredibly helpful.

Where do you create your first samples?

I create all the toiles and sometimes samples in-house. After the sampling is done, I hire technicians and seamstresses. All sampling gets made in the studio in London so I can have a close dialogue with the seamstresses to get the shapes right straight away.

Where do you manufacture your collection for production?

In the UK, but we are looking into where it would be beneficial for us to do production.

How do you present the collections to the clients?

I present during London Collections: Men for Menswear Fashion Week. I also have an agent who has a showroom in Paris, but most of the clients' and stylists' requests come from my website.

Who do you work with for selling the collection?

I recently started working with Alex Hidalgo, who has the Sifr Studios. Until now the label has been exclusive to Browns and been mainly showing during London Collections: Men, so I am very excited about the future with Alex.

Do you collaborate with other companies under your own label?

There have been talks about it, but I have so far done work for other people instead of under my label. I'm trying to keep them separate until it feels like something beneficial to the label in more than just a financial aspect. I have done collaborations with artists, filmographers, and musicians. It has been a learning curve that turned out to be extremely gratifying; people like these inspire me to continue to evolve into something better.

Interview: Felipe Rojas Llanos

1

Collections and their influences

It is possible to group or identify common themes in fashion that influence the creative process in developing a collection or how we choose to wear clothes. Recurring influences favored by designers at all levels of the market fall into four distinctive areas: historical, cultural, political, and environmental—all of which reflect the way we live globally.

Each new collection can explore a subtle redefinition of these recurring influences through the use of color, fabrics, proportion, and juxtaposition. Many designers establish successful brands based on a visual identity through a particular type of clothing or political view that represents their signature or reinforces brand values. This chapter provides some examples of designers' sources and influences in designing collections.

Although by no means an exhaustive list, it illustrates how designers respond to collective influences and translate them into a fashion reality that reflects their own design identity. It does not seek to identify consumer groups or particular fashion tribes or subcultures, but it focuses instead on some of the sources of creative fashion and those designers renowned for defining a particular identity or style.

1   Giambattista Valli, S/S 2014.

BACKGROUND

Every season, designers strive to develop their signature look or visual identity through their collections. Often they reference a number of sources and influences relevant to the current global, political, and social climate. For example, the emergence of deconstruction and reconstruction is evident during times of recession, such as in the early 1990s and during the economic downturn of the late 2000s. New, radical directions in fashion are often a reflection of, or a reaction to, the excesses of the time.

The glamorous, hedonistic, luxurious look of the 1980s was led by the late Italian designer Gianni Versace, the "King of Excess." This upwardly mobile period in fashion allowed women to "dress for success." Of course, other designers reacted to these excessive styles. Rei Kawakubo's Comme des Garçons collection caused a strong negative reaction in the early 1980s: her startlingly avant-garde, all-black collection in Paris was famously called "Hiroshima Chic" by the press. The Antwerp Six and Martin Margiela were inspired by this reactionary approach to design, and their unique methods of deconstruction continued to influence fashion throughout the 1990s in a direct reaction to the excesses of the time.

Vivienne Westwood references historical costume in her collections and subverts tailoring to create a new silhouette through reconstructing and modifying the structure of the body. Her use of tartan is legendary, from the early bondage trousers to the distorted tailoring of recent collections. At her studios she has an archive spanning thirty years of key pieces from her collections; these are revisited and reused by her design team for future collections. Similarly, Belgian designer Raf Simons has brought a new direction to Dior, revisiting the archive and bringing a stricter line and modernity to the house that reflects the current times.

2   **Alexander McQueen, Horn of Plenty, A/W 2009/10. The late Alexander McQueen often referenced historical events in his collections, with death and decay representing his darker side. Discovered by the late Isabella Blow, he dedicated his "Highland Rape" collection to her; it was based on landowners in Scotland forcing crofters out of their homes, as represented through the torn tartan. As always, the theater of the actual show reinforced the narrative.**

THE ANTWERP SIX

"A gang of fresh new fashion talents is determined to put Belgium on the map." —*Elle* US, 1988.

The original six designers to bring Belgian fashion to the forefront were Dries Van Noten, Ann Demeulemeester, Dirk Bikkembergs, Dirk Van Saene, Walter Van Beirendonck, and Marina Yee, who all graduated from the famous Antwerp Academy of Fine Arts. The strict four-year training, with its origins in Parisian haute couture, encouraged them to look inward on a journey to self-expression. According to their course director Linda Loppa, "the designers were all original but shared the same perfectionism."

MARTIN MARGIELA

A contemporary of the Antwerp Six, Margiela also graduated from the Antwerp Academy of Fine Arts. He launched his label Maison Martin Margiela in 1988 and challenged the fashion world with his conceptual approach and presentation of collections. Margiela, who has since left the label, was famous for not giving interviews and for a distinguishing feature of his collections: the catwalk show where all models have their faces concealed with masks and scarves.

3 A model presents a creation by Belgian Designer Martin Margiela for Maison Martin Margiela during the S/S 2011 ready-to-wear collection show on October 1, 2010, in Paris.

5 Norwegian Designer Peter Dundas's dark sophistication is favored by fashion editors Carine Roitfeld and Anna Dello Russo.

4 A model wears a "Palazzo" pajama outfit designed by Emilio Pucci.

Collections and their influences

HISTORICAL

Designers often look back to previous collections for inspiration. In particular, the original aesthetic of a well-established label may be revisited decades later, with collections referencing the same design, influences, and detailing. For example, Italian nobleman Emilio Pucci was popular throughout the 1960s (and again during the 1980s) for his use of wild, colorful patterns taken from Renaissance paintings, filigree, feathers, animals, stained glass windows, and ceramic tiles. He designed simple belted dresses, bodysuits, boat neck tops, and pants in silk jersey. These iconic, bold prints continue to be referenced today, with creative directors such as Matthew Williamson bringing the label up-to-date for the modern consumer.

Another example is Nicolas Ghesquière at Balenciaga. Ghesquière has since been appointed as Marc Jacobs's successor at Louis Vuitton, but while at Balenciaga, he continued Cristóbal Balenciaga's reputation for challenging the definition of aesthetics

through a combination of strong silhouette, color, proportion, and fabrics. His interpretation of the founder's original vision has been internationally applauded as a considered way of redefining fashion; it is evidence that inquiry and intellectual content in fashion can be colorful and dramatically beautiful. Ghesquière sketches initial ideas that inspire the cloth, cut, and shape of his garments.

Established designers, such as Karl Lagerfeld for Chanel and Alber Elbaz at Lanvin, continue to reference the fashion houses' iconic statements, playing with scale, logos, and accessories. Marc Jacobs's final collection for Louis Vuitton, for example, was an homage to every past collection. Key looks were represented in black as a memorial to his years designing for the house. Such designers continue to update the signatures of the past in glamorous and sensationalist garments, and they change direction from season to season or combine additional source materials and influences to refresh their signatures or styles. It is useful to see how other designers derive influences; it will in turn help to inspire you and enable you to analyze and reflect on your own thoughts, preferences, and creative identity.

6 A picture taken July 18, 2006, at the Paris Textile and Fashion Museum shows outfits exhibited at a retrospective of Spanish Designer Cristóbal Balenciaga. The exhibition ended January 28, 2007.

7 Balenciaga by Alexander Wang, S/S 2014.

Historical

CULTURAL

Since the 1960s international travel has become affordable and accessible to the majority of the developed world. This has broadened our knowledge and greatly influenced how we furnish our homes, our choices in the foods we eat, and how we dress. Ever since Yves Saint Laurent first showed the Moroccan Djellaba in the 1970s, designers and fashion consumers have understood the value and attraction of exotic, unusual garments, fabrics, and accessories. Designers play with juxtaposition, color, or multicultural references; garments such as the Scottish kilt, Indian sari, Chinese cheongsam, and Japanese kimono, have been continuously redefined in fashion collections. Folklore and ceremony provide a wealth of information that can inform fabric design—such as tartan, ikat embroidery, paisley, prints, and jacquards—as well as jewelry, footwear, and accessories. Some designers have developed distinctive identities based on the celebration of international, cultural references for garments, fabrics, color, and surface decoration.

Two such examples are Kenzo and Dries Van Noten. Kenzo has championed the multicultural narrative, placing Russian floral prints, for example, alongside brightly colored tartans and Norwegian snowflake knitwear graphics. Control of shape, silhouette, and color is a hallmark of Kenzo's work. The Kenzo style is clearly identifiable, influential, and has remained constant for over twenty-five years. Dries Van Noten reworks ethnic influences, traditional textile techniques, and coloration into the modern wardrobe. His love of ancient folklore and definition of adornment is carefully colored from the somber, urban uniform to the most colorful, embellished evening pieces, using images and treatments inspired by a range of ethnic crafts. Internationalism, folklore, and ethnicity continues to excite and contribute to many fashion collections. Examination of most designers' work will reveal the evidence of global influences.

8 Models wearing the new fall collection of fashion designer Yves Saint Laurent.

CONCEPTUAL

The origins of contemporary, conceptual fashion may well be credited to the Japanese designers Rei Kawakubo, Yohji Yamamoto, and Issey Miyake. For decades, these designers have been producing the most intriguing, provocative fashion by creating new ways of cutting and constructing. Conceptual collections are often beautiful, timeless, ageless, and dislocated from most visual narratives; however, they can also be too challenging, abstract, or unrelenting in identity, diminishing their influence on fashion trends. Designers Hussein Chalayan, Helmut Lang, and Jil Sander are all known for a minimalist, exacting aesthetic, which owes much to the rigors and precision of innovative architecture and reductive product design. There is usually little or no decoration to obscure the essence of the proportions, cut, finish, or quality of fabrics used. Beauty derives from the garments' core components and construction.

9

9 Creations by award-winning designer and Creative Director of Puma, Hussein Chalayan, are displayed at the Design Museum on January 21, 2009, in London, England.

"Hussein Chalayan is not just a fashion designer. His interests range across many disciplines; his work crosses so many boundaries."

—DONNA LOVEDAY

10 A model presents a creation by designer Hussein Chalayan during London Fashion Week, February 16, 2000.

10

HUSSEIN CHALAYAN

Hussein Chalayan trained as an architect before studying fashion at Central Saint Martins, London. Known for his conceptual collections and intellectual approach, he buried his graduate collection to see how it would decompose. Chalayan's collections reflect his explorations into product design and aircraft engineering: he created a jumbo jet dress that spread its wings, and he has made dresses grow and disappear through technology.

One of his most famous collections was "Afterwards" of Autumn/Winter 2000, which featured a set of 1950s furniture in a white room. The models dressed in the furniture covers, and a wooden table transformed into a skirt; this has since become an iconic statement of Chalayan's conceptual aesthetic. Chalayan now consults for global sportswear brand Puma, which has been influential in bringing in conceptual designers to consult on niche collections.

Conceptual

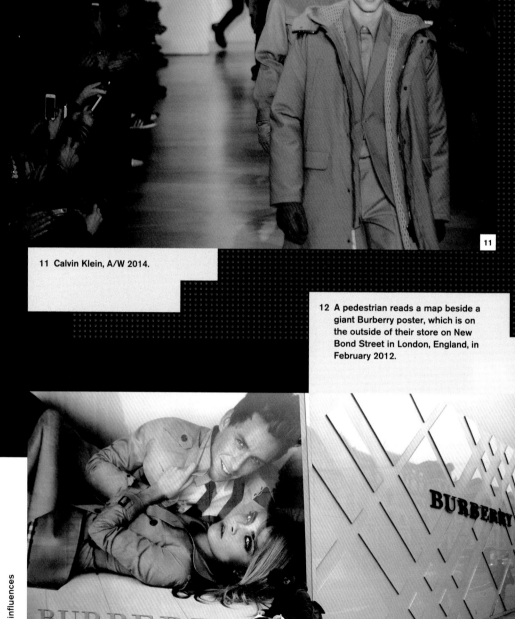

11 Calvin Klein, A/W 2014.

12 A pedestrian reads a map beside a giant Burberry poster, which is on the outside of their store on New Bond Street in London, England, in February 2012.

FUNCTIONAL

Functional garments, such as military wear and expedition clothing, have long influenced fashion designers. Menswear in particular continues to reference iconic military garments, workwear, and utility clothing, updating them in fabric, color, and details.

Military clothing has informed fashion partly due to the performance and ergonomic considerations of the wearer's activities and environment, as well as its overall look. This consideration has attracted a number of designers, such as Robert Cary-Williams, whose army background influenced his earlier collections for color and silhouette. Specifics such as camouflage have created an entire fashion agenda, involving recoloration and reapplication in unexpected contexts. The outcome may be as simple as Calvin Klein showing a military-inspired parka worn over a neat, single-breasted suit, with a shirt and tie. This exemplifies how a number of designers derive their inspiration and have created influential and successful fashion brands.

Often one item of clothing emerges and creates a new fashion descriptor. The safari jacket, the riding jacket, the cargo pant, and the biker jacket are all examples of this type of fashion transition. Occasionally, a garment defines an entire fashion category of its own, such as the Barbour, a waxed cotton shooting/fishing jacket that has become an iconic fashion statement in its own right. Another example is the trench coat; British companies Aquascutum (who pioneered the first waterproof gabardine) and Burberry (who launched the first trench coat after clothing the British army during the First World War) continue to produce these traditional "foul weather" garments but have updated them to satisfy today's fashion-conscious consumer. The trench coat is now considered to be a fashion wardrobe staple and has itself been the inspiration for jackets, dresses, evening wear, and childrenswear.

13

13 Michael Kors, S/S 2014.

Functional

14 From a Workers for Freedom collection: a British fashion label that was launched in 1985 by Graham Fraser and Richard Nott as a reaction against the "preppy" menswear styles of the period.

14

15 Perret workwear.

Workwear

The originator for workwear as a source and aesthetic is arguably Levi Strauss, who in the late 1800s created the first work overalls using twill cotton from Nimes, in France. This twill cotton—denim—has since been popularized by nearly every known designer and an infinite number of manufacturers across the world. In music, films, politics, youth culture, and high-end fashion, denim is used as a base upon which unlimited fashion stories can be created. The cloth's traditional construction details can be reworked with endless possibilities; it is ageless, global, and accessible to every social group. When asked if there was a garment he wished he had created, Yves Saint Laurent answered "the blue jean."

Claire McCardell who studied at what is now Parsons School in New York took a democratic approach to fashion by utilizing workwear, everyday garments, and childrenswear during the 1940s. This reaction to the American way of copying Paris fashions positioned her as one of the most influential designers of the twentieth century. Using workwear fabrics, such as denim, ticking, gingham, and calico, she produced clean utilitarian functional design classics.

16 A/W 2014-Acne-043.

Functional

Fashion reflects society, and designers will often reference political change in their collections. Messages through the clothes that we wear can be subversive or can be a bold statement to create a reaction. Katharine Hamnett famously did this when she invented the slogan T-shirt in the 1980s. These now iconic T-shirts were basic white with large, bold black lettering featuring sociopolitical messages such as antiwar statements. She intended for her slogans to be copied and read by people all over the world. Hamnett has now moved on to the global problem of ethics in the fashion manufacturing process; she is one of the designers responsible for introducing organic cotton to the masses.

Ethics and sustainability have become one of the main political agendas in fashion since the beginning of the new millennium. A number of designers have set up ethical labels certified by the World Fair Trade Organization (WFTO), such as People Tree. Larger companies are becoming influenced by emerging trends in recycling, upcycling, ethics, and diversity and are using organic fabrics in their collections.

Designers collectively have a common strength of purpose to challenge convention and break new ground in response to current affairs. For example, Jeremy Scott, whose first Paris collection was made of hospital gowns, sets out to provoke people with his collections that convey a message, an idea, or a thought.

Stella McCartney believes that fashion is political on a daily basis, and it is "about people expressing themselves through what they choose to wear." She is passionate about animal rights and refuses to include fur or leather in her collections.

Jean-Charles de Castelbajac uses political references in addition to his fine-art influences and translates these through humor in his colorful collections. His Spring/Summer 2009 collection included a knitwear piece that featured an image of Barack Obama, the first African American president of the United States; the bold statement reflected the changes in American society.

Caryn Franklin, OBE, has launched All Walks beyond the Catwalk to embrace diversity and promote use of models from all walks of life on the catwalk at London Fashion Week (LFW) with the support of Rankin.

17 **Obama dress by Jean-Charles de Castelbajac, A/W 2009.**

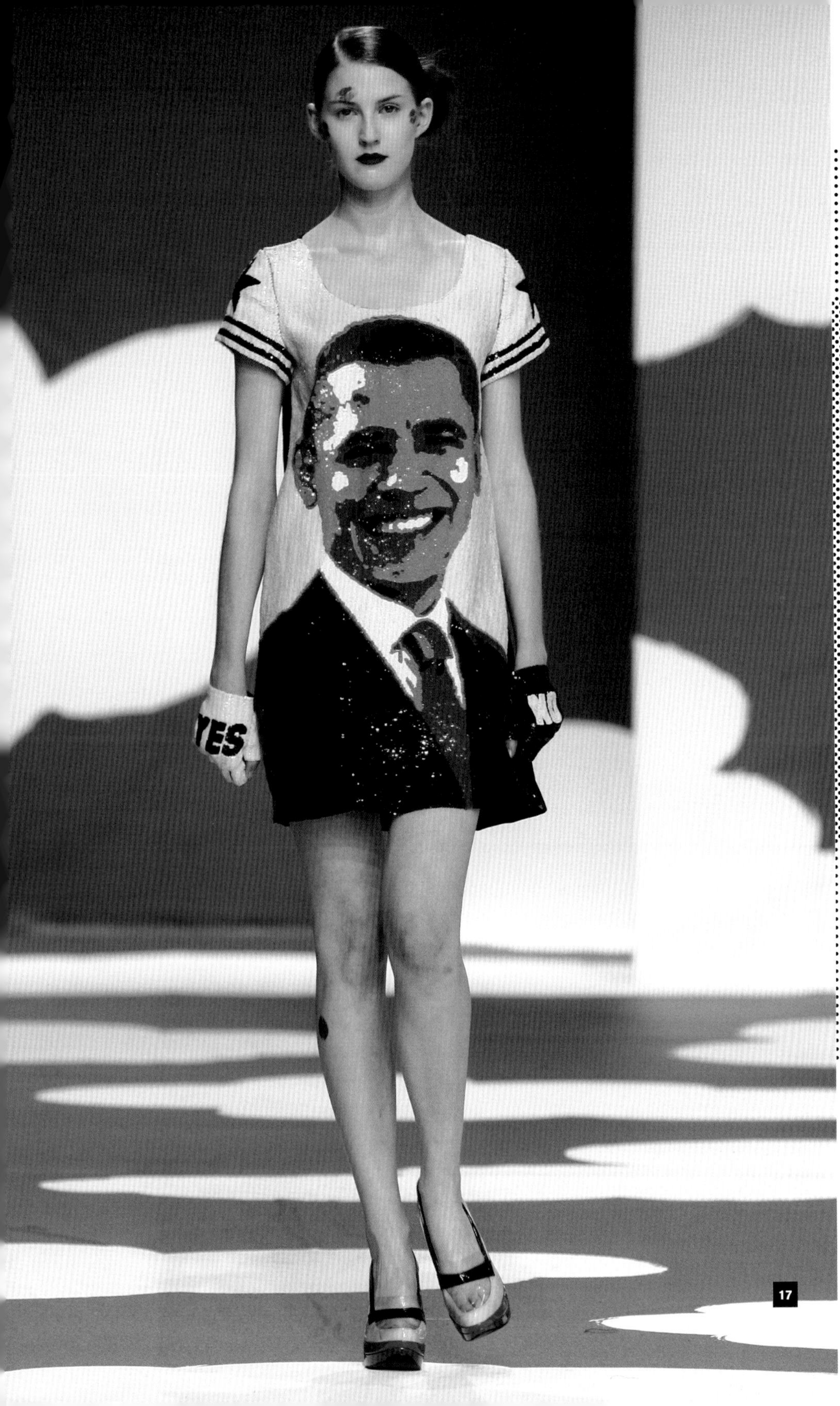

17

FUTURISTIC

The US designer Geoffrey Beene is regarded as a futurist: in the late 1990s, he decided to no longer use historical references on the basis that too many designers are overly dependent on them, restricting their development as innovative designers. He was responsible for redefining modern womenswear as we know it today.

In the 1950s and 1960s French Designer Pierre Cardin, along with his contemporaries André Courrèges and Paco Rabanne, designed futuristic, space-age fashion, which referenced science fiction rather than historical and traditional sources. Futuristic fashion can be obvious in its presentation (such as space-age clothes), but more importantly, it is about breaking new ground, taking fashion in a new direction.

For example, Cardin was the first couturier to launch a ready-to-wear line, and he was subsequently expelled from Chambre Syndicale de la Haute Couture in Paris. This represented the future of fashion as reflected by the demands of society. Similarly, a few decades earlier in the 1920s, feminist Coco Chanel broke new ground when she emancipated women from the restricting corsets of the Edwardian period. Today's designers are no less radical. Menswear designer Aitor Throup creates his clothes from his exquisite illustrations. His work is futuristic in approach: he draws out the characters and converts them into a wearable version. By not focusing on design details, he is freed up to produce a truly original final product. Gareth Pugh has evolved and refined the futuristic aesthetic displayed in his graduate collection. His exquisite pieces combine strong silhouettes and bold color, which represent the future of fashion today.

"I've always hated the idea of a retrospective: I don't like looking backwards, only going forward."

—GEOFFREY BEENE

18 Pierre Cardin's futuristic aesthetic.

19 Gareth Pugh, A/W 2014.

Collections and their influences

Designers have long been influenced by and collaborated with artists. Schiaparelli, who saw herself as an artist rather than a dressmaker, collaborated with Salvador Dali and Jean Cocteau in her surrealist-inspired collections. Dressing the then Duchess of Windsor, she created the iconic lobster dress with drawing by Dali. Similarly, Yves Saint Laurent (YSL) was influenced by Dutch abstract painter Mondrian, who used a limited palette of five colors for his color blocked paintings, which YSL reproduced on his 1960s shift dress.

When Marc Jacobs was Creative Director at Louis Vuitton (LV) he collaborated with a series of artists to reinvigorate the iconic monogrammed LV luggage. The first, in 2002, was the late fine artist Stephen Sprouse. In 2012 Japanese artist Yoyoi Kusama's signature polka dots in yellow and red covered the LV accessories in line with her Whitney Museum retrospective. UK designer Kim Jones, Menswear Styling Director at Louis Vuitton, also collaborated with contemporary artists Jake and Dinos Chapman who designed leopard-etched fox prints for his new menswear line.

Miuccia Prada, always the intellectual designer, used paper cutouts of a compilation of graphic artists and illustrators, including Gabriel Specter, Stinkfish, Pierre Mornet, Jeanne Detallante, and Henri Matisse, for her fun fur coats for Spring/Summer 2014, while minimalist designer Phoebe Philo introduced wild brush-stroke prints inspired by a combination of Hungarian photographer Brassaï's graffiti images and Parisian street-style art.

20 **A multicolored pop-art style summer fur coat by Micciu Prada, S/S 2014.**

Collections and their influences

FIONA STUART,
Co-owner and
Partner of Rellik

What and where did you study?
I did a Foundation course at Central Saint Martins in 1988/89, followed by a degree at Kingston in Interior Design.

How did you start sourcing vintage clothes?
I used to buy vintage clothing for fun but really starting sourcing to sell nineteen years ago. I had started selling a stall at Portobello Market. Originally I was selling new designer samples and collections but changed to vintage as that was what my customers were looking for.

Where do you source garments?
Fast forward nineteen years, my vintage sourcing and business has changed. Now I sell from people that approach the shop to sell. I also look at auctions, vintage fairs, and even other countries. eBay is a great global source for everything you need to look for. Now I am looking for the best, not the bulk, so my price point is higher too. Vintage is not the throwaway commodity it was fifteen years ago. Everyone knows its value or can research via the Internet.

When did you open your first shop?
I opened my first shop in 1999. I opened it with two other business partners from Portobello Market. It made sense to take the magic from the market but place it at a fixed address.

Do you have special conditions for storing?
Storage is always a battle between space and budget. I have preferred to store in heated spaces, preferably in my house. But storage units are now well-kept and organized. I believe you should keep clothes in garment bags, or storage rails covers, with rails elevated off the ground. Fragile and delicate items should be folded between tissue paper in trunks or boxes. Everything should be cleaned first. My secret was bulk dry cleaning. Everything is put through the machine but not pressed. I struck a deal with my local dry-cleaning company near my house. Hangers are important, too, as most of the damage is from them, not moths.

How many pieces do you buy a year?

At a guess I must buy about 6,000 to 7,500 items a years, including clothing, accessories, and jewelry.

Are the collections seasonal or by period?

I just buy on my instinct, great items to buy rather than by seasons or periods. You just feel that the item is interesting and that you should buy it. Often it might be another year until you actually put it out to sell. Usually I buy on-trend.

Which decade sells currently?

I would say that the '80s and now '90s sells best.

Which designer sells the best?

I would say Yves Saint Laurent, Hermès, Alaïa, and Jean Paul Gaultier. There are always others, depending on the current trends.

What is the price range in your shop?

The price range is from £25 to £550.

What has been your favorite piece?

There are a few favorites. From a Thea Porter silk caftan, a Versace embellished print dress, to my Galliano frock coat. Vintage is easy to love as you know you won't see another piece again.

Who buys your collections?

Everyone from collectors to museums, but mostly designers.

Do you sell through other stores?

Rellik has only sold in other stores through collaborations. There [were collaborations] with Selfridges, On Pedder, and LL-CC. Personally I often sell other items through other businesses if the item is better suited to their customers. To survive in business now, you need to be diverse.

Do you sell online?

Rellik does not sell online currently—but watch this space; it may change in the future.

Interview: Fiona Stuart

LOU AMENDOLA,
Chief Merchandising Officer
at Brooks Brothers

How do you start your collections?

We are not a fashion-forward company, but we are customer-driven. First we analyze how product lines perform, what sold, and why, such as fit of garment. We study trading reports and are influenced by the sales history: for example, a dress season can affect the sales of skirts. Secondly, we will be inspired by archive designs from 190 years of trading as a heritage brand. Thirdly we are influenced by global trends. The design team will visit Première Vision and catwalk shows to get trends and forecasts together with looking at the history of Brooks Brothers.

How many collections do you design?

We have four major deliveries in our main range: fall, holiday, spring, and summer. We have two deliveries in fall and only one in summer. A delivery can be from 100 to 200 styles. For Thom Browne, current guest designer on the Black Fleece range, we have two collections each with fifty styles in total.

How many are in the design team?

Ten in total, led by the creative director, with guest designers for specialist ranges, such as Thom Browne for the Black Fleece range, Junya Watanabe for a reinterpretation of the classic Brooks Brothers button-down shirt range. Designers work as part of a three-pronged attack: merchant plus designer plus product developer.

Do you compile a color palette?

We use classic colors for our foundation palette supplemented by colors from trend services, Première Vision and Pitti Filati. Our V-neck sweater for men will be produced in thirty colors.

How and where do you source fabrics?

Up to 50 percent are sourced in Italy, the remainder from Japan.

Where do you make your first samples?

The first samples are made in the factories where they are produced. Tech packs are produced by the technical department, who also produces patterns and first samples. We also have a tie factory, where fabrics are sourced from Italy and England.

Collections and their influences

How do you produce new shapes and silhouettes?

The design team develops new shapes based on existing styles. The process evolves rather than producing revolutionary new shapes—for example, slim-fit shirts, if the trends are for a slimmer silhouette.

Do you commission knit, print, and embroideries for the collections?

Knitwear is sourced from outside services, based on sketched details. Prints are designed from our own archive.

How many second lines do you produce?

Brooks Brothers has a manufacturing division for uniforms for hotels, airlines, and the military.

How do the designers communicate their ideas for the new collections?

They work to a designer brief, which is a road map for the direction of the collection. They will work closely with the merchants for styling and sampling. The designs then go into work in the form of samples. They are taken to an adoption meeting where designers and merchants will work for days putting together the collection of fifty styles that will be bought for the stores.

How do you promote the collection?

We spend 50 percent more than other companies in advertising and promotion. We produce a catalog and lookbook to promote each collection. The Brooks Brothers customers are loyal to the brand and feel part of the family. We have store events and e-mail customers for their feedback. Brooks Brothers is known as the place you were taken to for your first blazer, so there is a sentimentality associated with the brand, similar to Tiffany & Co., representing generations of style.

Interview: Lou Amendola

DR NOKI,
Fashion Designer and Artist

It's that line of rejection that seemed very intriguing. My brand identity had left me; I was not content.

Collections and their influences

Where did you study?
Edinburgh Art College, circa '89.

What did you do when you graduated?
I left Edinburgh in '93 and took myself to New York via Brighton, then to London to work in '95. NYC then was at the tail end of its utter wild years, when the Meatpacking District definitely didn't have cupcakes and boutiques. London is going through the same at the moment. When I first arrived, Shoreditch was an empty arena; now it's gone completely gladiatorial. To be a new graduate is an exciting thing in fashion; textiles will be going nowhere. We all need fashion, but it is style that has grace.

How did you set up your own label?
Setting up Noki was not a conscious decision, it happened through a frustration that I wasn't happy with the career paths available, the industry; fashion and art are very tricky. They applaud originality but boo its invention.

How do you research your collections?
I see them as a series of installations that culminate in bringing myself closer to a happier connection to the entertainment I enjoy the most: fashion, art, and humor. Something that is rooted very much in a landfill reality but creates a fantasy that lets me totally forget it's there . . .

How many collections do you design a year?
I don't see Noki in collections; it's all one big investigation garment by garment. I do not want Noki to have the constraints that a generic fashion collection creates. It has no pattern, just a collage of already produced garments.

The installations sustain the evolution of a new brand called Dr Noki NHS on the Fashion East runway. It creates only one-off pieces, the beginnings of a new dimension in fashion as couture called street couture, where its very sustainable canvas defines its originality in design. A code book, to a certain style defined, during our time in our new millennium, Noki is all about craft and form.

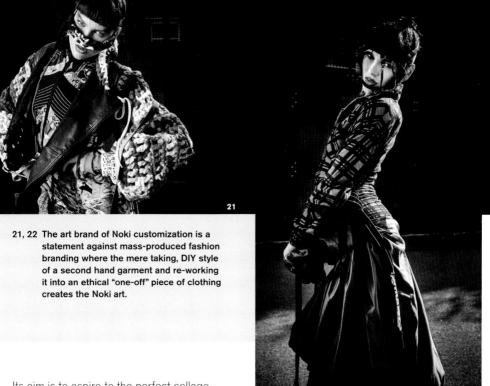

21

21, 22 The art brand of Noki customization is a statement against mass-produced fashion branding where the mere taking, DIY style of a second hand garment and re-working it into an ethical "one-off" piece of clothing creates the Noki art.

22

Its aim is to aspire to the perfect collage, making observations and documenting their beauty, investigating their power.

How do you compile your color palette?

The source for me is always the rag pile—its intense reflection, a rejection of color, weight, and weave. It redefines luxury as a random intervention.

How do you source your base cloths?

I am very lucky with the random rag intervention, Traid, LMB (London), Dirty Harry (Brighton), and kind donations. They all open their doors for inspiration. When you live and breathe a life, it either feeds or offends you.

How do you design your prints?

As an artist, I'm always drawing, working with pens, cutting collages. Creating fresh prints with Dr. Taz in the Norfolk studio is always a brilliant production moment. We now have an archive of screens that allows us to print collage the one-off print. Social networking outlets like Instagram have been another source of print ideas.

How do you develop your silhouettes?

Pattern cutting and silhouette are one of a kind. You really do have to understand the firm and form of the body proportion to cut into it. You need to be objective about how it can be redefined. You can only get that from constant subtle observations. Building a style of your own takes courage because it rejects trend but is the most important trend. You need to believe your style is the silhouette of the future.

Interview: Dr Noki

KATIE GREENYER,
Creative Director of
Red or Dead

How do you research?

We start off by having a gut feeling on trends that have been cropping up at catwalk shows and looks that key stylists have been pushing. We look at sales figures and see what styles are doing well. We look at trend predictions, such as The Future Laboratory, but usually our instincts are right. We look at WGSN (fashion and style forecasters) reports to see if there is anything we haven't covered, plus to see what other brands are up to.

We visit galleries and flea markets across the UK and Europe—Russia, China, you name it. If it is key to our trends, we will try and get there and experience it for ourselves. We research by going to films, exhibitions, libraries, and galleries. We all have cameras and make inspiration boards each week using what we have seen and done. We then publish these boards to all the product teams.

We are really our own trend agency. We also have an archive collection of products, sketches, [and] styles, which we revert to quite regularly. We do have a problem storing everything, so we tend to photograph it all before it goes off to a warehouse. Our inspiration boards contain fabrics, details, and anything that we can chop off and stick on for reference.

How many do you have in your design team?

The Red or Dead design team is small, but with all our licensing partners we have become quite big. We all work together, having inspiration days so that everyone is picking up on the same stories and vibes. It's great getting together and having product knowledge from each different category.

Where do you produce your samples?

In the Far East, India, and Europe.

How do you compile your color palettes?

From our inspiration and trend boards. We use Pantone references and fabric cuttings for dyeing. We normally produce four inspiration boards: color, shape, print, and graphics.

How do you present the collections?

We will do a presentation of all the range and produce a trend guide for inspiration, color, and packaging for the sales team. We show at Bread & Butter in Barcelona, Basel Watch Fair in Switzerland, Mido in Milan, and at Pure London.

How and where do you source your fabrics?

You have to follow the trends and inform the factories what you are looking for; the factories then send swatches to select from. As well as this, the design team visits fabric trade shows and markets for suitable fabrics.

Do you commission textiles, such as knit, print, embroidery, or weave?

No, this tends to be done in-house.

How do you develop silhouettes?

We research trends for the coming season looking at the catwalk and look on the high street to pick up on what people are wearing. It's then a matter of creating silhouettes and making them new and fresh and on-trend with a Red or Dead twist.

What do you define as a collection or range?

A collection is a range of garments that covers all product areas so that the consumer can be dressed head to toe in Red or Dead.

How many looks are in each collection?

We work to a phasing calendar that splits the collection up into mini collections. There are usually three to four phases with injection capsule ranges throughout the season to add newness. In each range they will be broken down into casual daywear, core, and eveningwear stories.

How many people work on each collection?

This is a mix of designers, product developers, and merchandisers, spreading out to buyers and the factories, who all play their own valuable parts.

How many pattern cutters do you have?

None in-house, but the product developers develop specs; they then work with the relevant factories to produce the patterns and garments. Each factory is specialized in specific products and therefore patterns.

Do you have in-house range reviews?

Yes, this is done at prototype stage to ensure that the product is working and is commercial, sits well as a collection, and shouts Red or Dead.

Do you work with PR teams?

We work with our PR agency. They work with all our different products, and we have regular launches and press days. So they are able to understand our brand, and we are able to feed the press samples and stories with just a phone call.

Interview: Katie Greenyer

SOPHIE HULME,
Fashion Designer

How do you start your collections?

I find stuff, old things I have collected and objects that I make into 3D garments, which I then sketch. I then design individual pieces rather than a whole look. I am not trend-led, but I build a wardrobe of key pieces that are designed to last. Each season I develop a new trinket, which collectively will form a giant charm necklace.

How many collections do you design each year?

I design in two-season brackets: Autumn/ Winter and Spring/Summer, which are aesthetically different with signature pieces running through. I don't have a big fashion show but have seen buyers from the beginning with lookbooks. Often they buy my pieces themselves, which is how my graduate collection was bought by Selfridges.

How many are in your team?

In my first season it was only me, but for this season, I have a freelance pattern cutter, a design assistant for specs and cutting, and some student helpers on work experience. I have a production manager for department store orders as I make to order, and if the stock is delivered a day late, the order can be canceled.

How do you compile a color palette?

I have a feeling about color and usually have a base of neutrals with a few accent colors, such as grays with aubergine. Sampling is limited, so I will swatch other colorways especially for buyers.

How and where do you source your fabrics?

I go to Première Vision in Paris and select stock fabric from mills and small companies in Italy, France, and Korea. I buy between 50 and 100 meters and commission colors. I also visit Linea Pelle in Bologna to source leathers.

Do you commission your own textiles?

I design my own prints and have them printed in repeat, and I have fabric sequined in India.

How do you develop your shapes and silhouettes?

I start working in 3D on the stand and don't use blocks.

How many samples do you produce?

I made twenty-five for the first Autumn/Winter season and thirty-five samples for Spring/Summer in a few colorways, as it is expensive to produce samples.

Do you have any sponsors or collaborate with anybody?

I have a PR called Cube but have no sponsors at present. I would like to collaborate with other people to produce special lines in future. I might possibly work in Japan with artists and go back to illustrating, which I only do for editorial at the moment.

Who are your stockists?

I showed at Rendez-Vous in Paris the first season, where Selfridges and b store in London bought my collection. I will also have my collection in the Convenience Store in London.

23 Sophie Hulme tote bag.

Interview: Sophie Hulme

KENNETH MACKENZIE,
Fashion Designer and Founder of Six Eight Seven Six

How do you start your collections?

My collections are personal and not largely defined but often use constant Six Eight Seven Six themes drawn from cultural and artistic influences. Six Eight Seven Six is always striving to go its own way and not be a slave to arbitrary trends and targets. Fundamentally, we aim to create clothing with design, longevity, and quality. This guiding principle drives us to develop an evolving wardrobe reinterpreting the classical confines of menswear by blending the latest fabric and manufacturing technology with proven traditional materials and construction. Taking inspiration from art, music, idealism, architecture, product design, and nature, we try and evolve an aesthetic that resonates with our lives and the lives of our customers. "We" is an important concept at Six Eight Seven Six, for while we are built round a central core, we are in essence a collaboration, with a shifting cadre of artists and outsiders. We don't really do collections now, although we use the same influences for research.

How many collections did you design?

From 1995 to 2008, we did two collections a year for Spring/Summer and Autumn/Winter, which we wholesaled to stores. We started by finding garments, mainly workwear and classic outdoor clothing and army surplus. We simplified the garments and took them into modern fabrication and I used that as a template to then design, evolving to create my own aesthetic.

From 2008 onward, the concentration has been on "rolling" product and collaborations sold from our own website.

How did you source your fabrics?

Première Vision. It wasn't always easy to find new forward-thinking fabrics and flexible suppliers, but by persevering we managed to find a way. In the early days, I didn't want to leave Première Vision without all the fabrics, but now I have become more relaxed and flexible in how we develop product, and the main aspect is to have a good relationship [with] manufacturers and fabric mills who understand your business.

How many garments did you make?

When we went to Première Vision, we took with us a collection in linear form of twenty to twenty-five pieces. We would find fabrics that would fit in two to three styles for minimum orders. Sometimes it didn't work because the factories found it difficult to make twenty-five styles in three different fabrics.

How did you develop shapes and silhouettes?

Influences were always similar and still are: classic menswear, military, and vintage sportswear. Accessories, such as shoes with Tricker's and Italian-made bags, were introduced around 1999/2000 and recently we've reintroduced them after a hiatus.

When did you change how you develop your collections?

I had a break from my business, designed for A Life in NY, and had a lifestyle change—bought a bike and went camping—then returned to the business in 2005. This time the ranges, rather than moderate collections, were more technical and mainly sportswear.

24 Kenneth MacKenzie
jacket, A/W 2013.

24

How many do you have in the design team?

I work with various freelance people to create the product and visual representation of the brand, but the actual garment design tends to be myself.

Where do you produce your garments?

In the past we manufactured in Italy, [and] Portugal, but now it's predominately the UK, with some of our collaborative work being made in Japan and Asia. This is mostly due to currency changes and the fact that if a brand finds the correct factory in the UK the minimums are much more acceptable, especially as Six Eight Seven Six is mostly sold online direct to the customer.

Do you collaborate with anyone?

Our early collaborations were around 2000 with the likes of Tricker's shoes in Northampton and then we rejected the twice-a-year seasonal format that provided the opportunity for me to consult for brands and work with more collaborators. So we worked with Fred Perry on a blank canvas for Laurel Wreath as I was designing that particular collection at the time, and we created a range of accessories called R6 with a Northamptonshire-based factory, which lasted for two years.

There've been numerous smaller collaborations, but the two constants recently have been Rohan the British outdoor brand and Cash Ca in Japan with Kazuki Kuraishi, which have both involved a real fusion of design and resources.

How do you sell and promote your ranges?

Six Eight Seven Six has never believed in the idea of advertising or fashion shows, so the advent of social media has been very helpful. We use our website, Facebook, Twitter, and Instagram, as well as good support from various blogs, which have replaced the excellent support we had in the early days from magazines.

Interview: Kenneth MacKenzie

WILL BROOME,
Fashion Designer and
Illustrator

How do you start your collections?

It varies from season to season. Working with a designer, such as Marc Jacobs, they might ask what I am developing at the moment. It is an organic process, and we collaborate through dialogue. There is a lot of time involved, as we are working in partnership because they know and like my work. I have been collaborating on the Marc by Marc [Jacobs] for six years. For Autumn/Winter 2004, I designed the multiple skull and panda prints for the womenswear collection and T-shirts for menswear. Then Wedgwood approached me to design their 250th anniversary china as they liked my style. They gave me carte blanche to work how I wanted. I felt it an honor to be asked by a heritage brand such as Wedgwood.

Describe your style of illustration.

Cute with darkness behind: cutouts, naive, mainly in black and white. I don't use a computer to generate my work, only to scan.

I choose to work with lack of precision and a return to the hand-drawn. I use paper stolen from the photocopier, pads of colored paper, and Berol fine liners (a red one for thick lines and turquoise for fine lines). I work in sketchbooks on the go and draw something every day. I used to get in trouble at school, but now I am a professional doodler!

How did you start?

I submitted A5 sketchbooks, which were used on the catwalk, the clothes, bags, and stickers on everything.

How many illustrations do you produce per season?

Usually twenty-five drawings maximum, which I collage to get a new image. Once they are sold, they are exclusive to Marc Jacobs.

25 Will Broome, selection of
illustrations.

26 Will Broome, Marc by
Marc Jacobs.

27 Will Broome,
Personal 1.

3

Designing for different markets

Within the global fashion industry, collections are designed for various market levels. At each level it is important to understand who the target customer is and how the collections will be presented and sold. To define the key areas of contemporary fashion, the following market levels should be noted: haute couture, prêt-à-porter or ready-to-wear, designer labels, luxury brands, high street, online, and home shopping.

This chapter introduces the different market levels, discussing how the collections are developed and how the design and development process differs at every level.

1   Dior, S/S 2014.

HAUTE COUTURE

Haute couture is the highest, most specialist market level. Couture is preindustrial fashion based around privately commissioned ateliers (workshops) producing handmade, bespoke garments fitted to clients who appreciate the highest quality and utmost privacy. Established houses, such as Chanel, Givenchy, Dior, and more recently Gaultier, are members of the Chambre Syndicale de la Haute Couture and show their couture collections in Paris over three days in January and July. Currently there are only twelve full members compared with over 100 in 1946. Only garments that are handmade in France, by members of the Chambre Syndicale de la Haute Couture, can be labeled as haute couture. But the Chambre may also invite guest designers, such as Martin Margiela, Valentino, and Giorgio Armani, to show alongside other members in Paris. In 2008 Boudicca, the English design duo, were honored with an invitation to show during Paris Haute Couture Week.

CHAMBRE SYNDICALE DE LA HAUTE COUTURE

This was the initiative of the first known English couturier Charles Frederick Worth. Couture houses that are members of Chambre Syndicale de la Haute Couture must meet and maintain strict criteria, including specialist aspects of the manufacturing process and the location. All processes are controlled within the atelier or studio (which may sometimes just be the artisans working in their own homes).

The origins of haute couture

The origins of fashion or dress can be traced back to the early seventeenth century, when France was the center for luxury silk textiles in Europe. Aristocratic women would commission makers to produce personal gowns and accessories for social and court occasions. Makers, known as *couturiers* (from the French *couter*—to sew), would create one-off clothes for clients and include their names on labels sewn into the garments.

The atelier

Traditions continue with the couturiers of today. Within the atelier, which is usually owned by the design house, each garment type is created within a specialist area. The *flou* is an area specializing in dresses and draped garments. The *tailleur* focuses on tailoring for suits, jackets, and coats. The chief dressmaker is known as the *première* and assistants are apprentices. Couture houses are traditionally separated by skills into the flou and tailleur. However, with more money to be made in daywear than evening wear, the boundaries are now blurring.

For example, Karl Lagerfeld at Chanel commissions the dressmakers to work on unstructured jackets, which brings a lightness to the tailoring. Couture gowns rely on the craftsmanship of the ateliers, where specialist handwork is carried out to the designer's and client's specifications. The atelier is the laboratory for developing and maintaining new fabrics, beading, cutting, embroidery, and the highest level of handwork and finish. Chanel has bought five ateliers, including Lesage, which specializes in flowers, braids, and feathers. Other houses in Paris, such as Dior, also use this atelier. (Dior no longer owns its own specialist ateliers.)

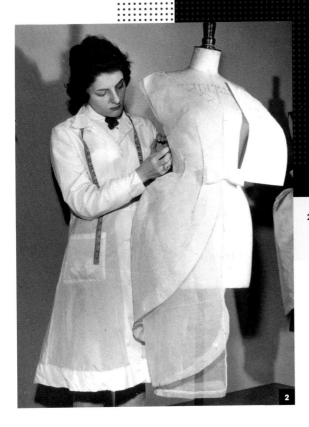

2 **Modeling on the stand.**

Developing a haute couture collection

Designers begin haute couture collections in much the same way as ready-to-wear. John Galliano, for example, starts his haute couture collection by drawing sketches and selecting fabrics. Each season, showing the couture collection allows potential clients the opportunity to see firsthand the possibilities for next season's wardrobe. Appointments are then made with the designer/house to attend private viewings and make individual selections. Clients buy close to the season, seeing a show in January for that spring (unlike ready-to-wear, which shows for the following season). This ensures exclusivity for the client, who values the privacy and service only available at this level of the market.

Then, after seeing the collection, a client will make an appointment with the *vendeuse* (saleswoman) in the salon. Having made a selection, the client must have the pattern adapted to ensure that the garments are personally fitted to their measurements and body proportions. A series of fittings will take place, using calico toiles. The toile records the exact cut, fit, and finish and will also detail information for linings, interfacing, and embellishments. The fittings and client selections are confidential and reflect the exclusive nature of this fashion market. Regular clients will, over time, have a personal form made to their exact measurements.

3 Chanel couture finale,
with Karl Lagerfeld, S/S 2014.

The future of haute couture

Due to the extremely high costs associated with the production and purchase of couture clothing and the growth in popularity of ready-to-wear, there are fewer customers able or willing to buy couture. Over the last twenty years, a number of designers have expanded into this level of the market, including Versace, only to retreat when the cost and competition have proven to be unworkable or unnecessary to develop the core business. Many couture houses have closed their ateliers, although the label may continue in accessories or fragrances. Changes in society mean that many of the traditional social formalities have disappeared, and there is less demand for this type of clothing. It is estimated that no more than 4,000 women across the world can afford to buy haute couture wardrobes, and the number of women who buy regularly is considerably smaller. As such, many designers

3

and fashion houses will loan evening gowns to young celebrities to freshen the image of couture. Celebrity events such as the Oscars and Golden Globes ceremonies in Los Angeles, Cannes Film Festival in France, and the BAFTA Awards in London are now important showcases for haute couture designers. Although many celebrities will still wear ready-to-wear to such events, there is an increase in couture dresses by Ellie Saab, Valentino, and Giorgio Armani Privé. During these occasions, the designers set up hotel workrooms to ensure that the clients have fittings right up to the event. High profile international professional women, royalty, and members of the aristocracy will wear haute couture as they value the privacy and bespoke fittings available at this level of the market.

Haute couture

READY-TO-WEAR

Ready-to-wear, or *prêt-à-porter*, covers any collection that consists of garments produced in volume—distinct from the one-off garments in haute couture. Couture is establishment and classic, whereas ready-to-wear is young and subject to trends and change. A ready-to-wear collection is created for a wider customer base and will be produced in standardized sizes. Ready-to-wear can span from established design houses, which also produce couture, to international and smaller designers setting up independent labels.

The origins of ready-to-wear

Couture houses first began to produce cheaper lines for their in-house boutiques in the 1930s. Then, after the Second World War, the couture houses established boutiques to cater to a changing world by offering off-the-rack collections, known as prêt-à-porter. These collections were based on their couture lines at an affordable price. Up until 1950, Italian and American fashions relied on Paris couture, and highly skilled dressmakers would copy designs. Early forms of licensing were established by couturiers, such as Christian Dior, who sold patterns and muslin toiles to the United States to be copied and sold in department stores.

After the death of Coco Chanel in 1971, Paris entered into a period of transition, and the couture houses were struggling against mass production in the UK. The couture houses reacted by offering affordable diffusion collections inspired by their couture styles. By the end of the 1970s, the House of Chanel had launched its own ready-to-wear lines and Dior launched Miss Dior. Haute couture continued to influence the designer's ready-to-wear collections in fabric, color, silhouettes, and theme.

Many aspects of design and products were being reconsidered and exciting design ideas dispensed with existing aesthetics and materials. In the 1970s Yves Saint Laurent launched Rive Gauche—ready-to-wear for women and men. The Rive Gauche collections popularized his avant-garde approach to style, luxury, and the contemporary fashion consumer. Based on the reputation of the hip Left Bank district of Paris, Saint Laurent created an enticing image of the modern consumer in touch with contemporary cultures—a global traveler who understood cultural and creative diversity and the courage to question convention. Saint Laurent successfully built an international fashion empire based on ready-to-wear, while creating shocking (for their time) fashion statements, including the safari suit and "Le Smoking"—a tuxedo-style suit for women. It could be argued that this look and many others from Saint Laurent provided the basic template for the modern women's wardrobe.

READY-TO-WEAR IN THE UNITED STATES

Ready-to-wear can be traced back to the beginning of the twentieth century, following the Industrial Revolution and the introduction of the sewing machine. Immigrants from Eastern Europe with tailoring skills settled in New York. They did piecework in their crowded tenements or worked in nearby factories, often in unsafe conditions for low wages, to service the growing population. After the First World War, companies began to visit the Paris shows and to buy patterns to copy for the American market using cut, make, and trim outfits in New York. By the end of the Second World War, this was replaced with licensing deals, which were less costly than buying couture samples to copy.

Designing for different markets

4   September 1969: The French couturier Yves Saint Laurent is flanked by Betty Catroux (right) and Loulou de la Falaise outside his new shop on New Bond Street, London.

> **The most important aspect of producing your own collection is to have a unique product that the customer will buy every season to ensure longevity.**

DESIGNER LABELS

Designer labels cover independent designers who set up their own business, either alone or with a partner. Having a business partner can be advantageous, as he or she can deal with the business plan, monitor accounts, and approach investors, thereby allowing the designer time to be creative. Start-up companies are usually funded by loans from banks, inheritance, or less often, by venture capitalists. Another option is to secure sponsorship through funding initiatives, such as British Fashion Council, New Gen sponsored by Topshop, Lulu Kennedy's Fashion East, Fashion Scout, or Fashion Fringe. In the United States the Council for Designers in America (CFDA) has established the Vogue Fashion Fund, offering endowments to the next generation of designers.

Often designers starting out on their own will not be able to afford employees beyond a freelance pattern cutter and sample machinist. In addition to creative skills, they will therefore also need to be flexible, tenacious, enduring, and prepared to work long hours, ensuring that their catwalk dream is realized and delivered to stores within a three-month period. The benefit of designing for one's own label is being able to develop your own signature with the hope of being picked up by the large French or Italian fashion houses or backed by a high-street company. The most important aspect of producing your own collection is to have a unique product that the customer will buy every season to ensure longevity. Having your own website and being engaged in social media can raise your profile, but a good product that is new, well made, and delivered on time within cost is essential to your survival.

5   Christopher Kane, S/S 2013.

Designing for different markets

The current fashion market covers product areas that extend far beyond clothing and personal accessories. Designers and retailers have created brands to define a lifestyle or design language that is communicated to consumers. As with other industries, this creates a demand based on want rather than need. In today's world, there are trends in every aspect of life, and we are all, to some extent, aware of what is fashionable.

Over the past twenty years, the designer ready-to-wear market has expanded to include an enormous range of labels, diffusion lines, accessories, and other branded products. Pierre Cardin was the first designer to expand into a range of fashion and non-fashion areas. Cardin designed and branded eyewear, fragrances, Cadillac cars, footwear, telephones—even chocolates. This expansion was ultimately perceived as diminishing the brand, with the result that the Cardin name became devalued and unfashionable.

Gucci suffered the same fate, coming to represent bad taste. Gucci reevaluated their heritage and prior status by canceling a large number of licenses and by appointing Tom Ford as Design Director to refocus ready-to-wear. Following his first ready-to-wear collections in the mid-1990s, Ford successfully repositioned Gucci as a global leader. His influence was used to redesign the Gucci store interiors, fragrance packaging, and editorial campaigns—collectively refining the company's position as a luxury fashion house.

When YSL was sold to the Gucci group in 2000, Ford applied the same approach to reinvigorate the YSL brand—again with acclaim; he repositioned YSL at the forefront of modern ready-to-wear fashion.

Currently, international ready-to-wear designers have businesses aimed at different levels of the market. Regardless of market niche, each branded collection is created and produced in the same way. The brand is clearly identified as targeting specific customers or occasions, while aiming to capture the designer's identity either through design or advertising. Pricing, fabrics, and finish are all used to differentiate each line.

International designers provide the main content for the ready-to-wear shows during the fashion week in the fashion capitals of New York, London, Milan, and Paris. In addition to the published schedules for these renowned shows, fashion weeks also take place across the world, in cities such as São Paolo, Melbourne, Shanghai, Tokyo, Madrid, Rome, and New Delhi. The fashion industry is international in consumer awareness, demand, production, and promotion, with brands such as Louis Vuitton, Gucci, Prada, and Dior being recognized, demanded, and available across the world.

6   Kate Moss, Gucci, A/W 1995.

7

7   Peter Pilotto for Target,
A/W 2014.

depend on price and creative alignment with the designer's main, more expensive collection. Some pieces can be cheaper versions of current or past season's pieces. The creative process is exactly the same as if the collection were in a higher market segment, with costs saved in the fabric choices, production volume, and profit margin at retail. Many retailers have identified the value and prestige of promoting a guest or celebrity designer to enliven and extend core ranges. This strategy creates opportunities for a new customer group and will also attract the designer's fans. In the United States, Target has pioneered this strategy, employing a diverse range of designers to create collections of clothing, homewares, and accessories. Isaac Mizrahi, Todd Oldham, Michael Graves, and recently Austrian fashion-print designer Peter Pilotto and his partner Christopher de Vos have all helped Target carve a distinctive and design-led profile among US retailers. Japanese company Uniqlo followed this trend and employed Jil Sander as its design consultant, and John Lewis carried a range by Alice Temperley.

Award-winning designer Giles Deacon has an extensive portfolio and is a prolific collaborator. His collaborations span across all market levels from New Look, Daks, Mulberry, and Nine West to Ungaro in Paris and haute couture for a number of celebrity clients. He has also collaboratively designed products for Sky, DFS, Converse, and Evoke jewelry. Giles, as he is known, was also sponsored by Norwegian water brand Isklar to design a charity tote bag for Oxfam.

DESIGNER COLLABORATIONS

Many retailers have designer ranges as part of their main merchandise. These ranges are manufactured to prices that are more widely affordable than the designers' main collections. In exchange for the designed range and use of the designer's name, the retailer will arrange the sourcing, fabrics, production, and visual promotion. This arrangement can be mutually beneficial and profitable for both parties concerned.

The collections are usually designed as capsule ranges, pieces that can be easily put together in whole outfits, or relaunches of archive pieces. Their appeal and success

Celebrity collaborations

Perhaps the most successful celebrity collaboration of recent times has been the partnership between Sir Philip Green, Owner of Topshop, and model and muse Kate Moss. Taking inspiration from her own wardrobe of vintage garments, Kate Moss directed an in-house team of designers. Although not trained or experienced as a designer, Moss has become a living fashion icon and is associated as being the face of a number of brands. Her status and profile is a match for many of the brands and designers who have used her image to promote and define their own products and collections. Similarly H&M launched collections by international pop royalty Madonna and Kylie Minogue, and more recently Beyoncé appeared in their campaigns.

8 Peter Pilotto, S/S 2014.

HIGH STREET

Across many mass-market or high-street retailers, each fashion collection or range is scheduled to be available in-store at prescribed times. Known as *drops*, the collections will be staggered into early and high season. This "fast fashion" offers the customer a changing retail experience, as subsequent items or stories will be delivered in a number of weeks. Most retailers will continue to offer core ranges that evolve from season to season, reflecting a more conservative customer or clothing area. Core ranges include men's suiting, separates, and accessories. Nightwear, underwear, and sweatshirt separates are also typical core lines, as these are much less influenced by high-fashion trends or directions. Many retailers aim to offer new ranges every two weeks, although this merchandise strategy is mainly featured within fashion-focused retailers such as H&M and Topshop. New ranges are displayed in-store as soon as delivery is received. The ranges are often promoted on the retailer's website or in the fashion press as news or "buy it before it goes."

MARKS AND SPENCER

UK company Marks and Spencer, and the other high-street chain stores that followed, were not design innovators but suppliers of basic goods. M&S began as a penny bazaar in Leeds and today has over 1,000 stores worldwide. Things began to change when Brian Godbold, head of design, employed Paul Smith as a design consultant. In the 1970s and 1980s the market became saturated with basic products, which in turn created a need for conspicuous design. M&S bought American brand Brooks Brothers in the 1980s but didn't become an influence in fashion until the Autograph range was launched in 2000, which really changed the company's profile. Designers Betty Jackson, Julien MacDonald, and Katharine Hamnett all designed upmarket capsule ranges that were to be sold anonymously under the Autograph label. M&S were also one of the first chain stores to support up-and-coming designers, funding Hussein Chalayan and Matthew Williamson for the BFC New Generation show at London Fashion Week in 1998.

The supplier

Only a few chain stores have in-house design teams. They rely on the design teams employed by their suppliers or manufacturers; these teams are usually specialists in their core product, such as jersey or men's tailored trousers. As a result, the buyer will essentially "design" or compile the collection by sourcing pieces from a number of suppliers. Increasingly, chain stores are using suppliers with factories in places where labor and fabric is cheap, such as Asia, South America, and Eastern Europe. The buyers will begin with a base color palette and mood boards to show their suppliers the intended theme for the collection. The suppliers will then provide samples and have weekly meetings with the buyers and merchandisers. Designers who work for suppliers have the opportunity to shop the world for sample garments.

In the UK, many factories were once "vertical," which meant they produced both the cloth and the finished garments. However, most of the mills and factories have now closed down due to increasing costs and competition from mass production overseas. Some factories will be commissioned to produce a range of garments for the overall collection, but this is rare. One exception is Spanish retailer Zara, which is a vertical producer. The company's business structure enables production of both fabric and garments, thereby allowing for complete flexibility in production and styles. With its own retail outlets, Zara is able to control every aspect of the design, production and retail chain, while keeping costs in control and stock change responsive to fashion direction and sales. Stock is therefore planned to offer ongoing choice, with the customer aware that the items may be sold out in a few weeks.

With the rapid and popular development of inexpensive, fast fashion, many consumers are now concerned about the ethics and sustainability of this market level. These concessions are being reflected in the emergence of retailers marketing eco-fashion as organic, fair trade, or socially responsible. This is a complex and challenging area for designers, manufacturers, retailers, and consumers. But as an increasing number of environmental and social factors are demanding that we reconsider how and why we consume fashion, along with a growing responsibility within the choices we make, this will undoubtedly change future considerations for fashion designers and consumers.

9 Per Una top and
skirt, from the Marks
and Spencer A/W
2015 collection, and
Marks and Spencer
collection coat and
jumper, A/W 2015.

DEVELOPING HIGH-STREET COLLECTIONS

For corporate branded companies with in-house design teams, the design process is similar to that in high-end fashion. The design team will start developing a new collection while still working on the previous one. Elements are often carried across, whether they are successful pieces from a previous collection or core pieces that sell every season. From their sourcing trips around the world, the design team will collate inspiration boards, or mood boards. These boards form an important basis for the design process, reinforcing the design team's vision for the new collection. Information pinned on the mood boards include color swatches, sketches, photographs, tear sheets, text, illustrations, fabric samples, and actual garments, which can be bought for fabric, color, and embroidery references.

Approximately three months before the design process begins, the fabric designers will visit mills to develop specially woven sample cloth known as *blankets*. Once sketches have been produced and edited, sample garments are made: first in an inferior cloth, such as cotton calico or muslin, and then in the sample cloth. Over the next few weeks silhouettes will be developed; this is an ongoing process and many pieces are discarded in favor of garments that reflect the mood of the season. And so begins the editing process, where approximately 40 percent of the original sample garments will be shown to the client or on the catwalk. As many as 150 pieces will be made, which represent around fifty looks or exits onto the catwalk or runway.

Designing for different markets

9

Once the garments have been shown there will be further adjustments to the collection by the merchandiser, who collaborates with the designer to finalize what to buy and in what quantities for their retail stores. The different ranges are displayed on large, portable grids, each representing drops or deliveries into store; this process is called *rigging* in the US and *range building* in the UK. Rigging can represent different color stories for different labels within the brand. They give buyers, merchandisers, and designers an overview of the collection. The editing process should involve distilling and refining looks into tight ranges, which represent the spirit of the overall collection.

TECH PACKS

Technical packages, or tech packs, are given to factories to produce prototypes for the collections. They usually contain specifications, measurements, fabric, trim, and lining information: basically everything needed to produce a garment in the factory.

ONLINE SHOPPING

Online shopping offers fashion consumers a huge range of merchandise across all brand and price levels. At the top end of the online market is Net-a-Porter, set up in 2000 by fashion journalist Natalie Massenet in a small flat in Chelsea with fifteen staff surrounded by boxes of stock. Part of Massenet's success can be attributed to her style and the luxurious black gift boxes delivered the next day.

Stella McCartney, Alexander Wang, and RM by Roland Mouret are among the designers who now design collections specifically for the site, having originally sold their main collections through the site. With its ability to buy pieces quickly from collections directly after the designer's catwalk show and showcase merchandise even before it is available in some stores, Net-a-Porter has revolutionized the way women shop. Up to two million women log on each month to browse through 200 leading labels.

Catering to a younger customer, ASOS (As Seen on Screen) has developed an online fashion business that, like a number of other e-tailers, limits availability and produces a large number of ranges across each traditional season. Ranges are designed and produced in a number of countries, and stock is carefully planned on prior sales and time for availability within the traditional buying timescale—Autumn/Winter becomes available during August and Spring/Summer comes online in January and February. The original concept was to copy and sell copies of celebrity looks or red-carpet fashion—ASOS is an acronym for "As Seen on Screen." The company has since evolved into a successful fashion-centered organization that strives to produce the latest fashion looks at competitive prices for men and women.

Home shopping

Before Internet shopping took off, home shopping was the option to buy merchandise through the mail. Originating in the late 1800s in the United States, the idea of home shopping was to capture the attention of a generation who did not live near retail shops. The twice-a-year Sears, Roebuck, and Co. catalog—one of the original catalogs—was expansive and covered an enormous range of products, including kit houses, home and lifestyle items, appliances, and mail-order chicks, as well as fashion. This company and many others became embedded as part of the American way of life; soon after, this form of shopping arrived in Europe and the UK.

Designing for different markets

By the 1950s, the clothing ranges presented in these catalogs were extravagantly illustrated or photographed, often in exotic or aspirational locations and settings. But while the clothing ranges were seasonal, they were made in large numbers, and stock size and quality were often average. Garments were designed to be only seen from the front, so the silhouette and backs of garments were basic and dull. This form of fashion production and retail was often considered dowdy or downmarket until entrepreneur George Davies launched the Next Directory in 1982.

The Next Directory transformed the notion of home shopping. Customers had to pay to receive a copy of the catalog, which was glossy and featured real fabric swatches alongside photographs and a measuring tape. This interactive experience, coupled with fashion photography by Bruce Weber featuring models from design magazine campaigns, transformed the idea of home shopping into something cool, informed, and exciting. The ranges were clearly influenced by fashion trends and current influential designers.

This was the first British retail organization to understand the concept of "total look" merchandise and styling. Some items might have been fairly basic, but the overall image and packaging created the desired halo effect for the high-street fashion consumer. For ten years the visual and merchandise format established by Next was influential in endless retail spaces and stores across the UK.

Interview

GILES DEACON,
Fashion Designer

How do you start your collections?

We start the next collection before we finish the one we are working on. For example, the Autumn/Winter 2009 research started three weeks before the Spring/Summer 2009 show. We need to keep up the pace in the studio, as certain staff are on a monthly salary, so we are producing all the time and do pre-collections as well. When researching for the new collection, I use stuff that has been collected all year round, and I work in sketchbooks.

How do you develop new shapes?

Patterns that haven't worked in the past are reworked. Cutters work on new shapes from inspirational mood boards; finishes may come from any surplus garments for new fabrics. I also set mini projects for assistants and students who will go around the shops looking at how garments, such as those at Prada and Lanvin, are made. The interpretations of new styles need to look like they come from Giles.

How many collections do you design?

There are eight in total: two main collections, Spring/Summer and Autumn/Winter for Giles; two pre-collections for July and November; and four collections a year for New Look.

How many are in your team?

There are nine full-time, four part-time, and a number of students.

How do you compile a color palette?

I do it instinctively, starting with core black and navy and adding a few new colors for trims. Choosing a color is not a major problem.

Where do you source your fabrics?

Japan and the UK, France for denim, lace from Austria, and I develop crêpe fabrics in UK mills who will produce thirty meters specifically for us.

How do you develop your prints and knitwear?

I have a long working relationship with designers Fleet and Rory, who interpret the feel of the collection or prints. Ideas develop in conjunction with the print designers. Rory works through drawings, and Fleet works texturally. Syd will work large-scale knitwear showpieces, and fine-gauge knitwear samples are made in Italy. We also use Swarovski crystals on embroideries and prints.

How do you communicate with your cutters?

I sketch ideas for our creative cutters who work on patterns and draping on the stand. They draw in cloth on the stand, working spontaneously, putting things on, and often create happy accidents that are made into toiles for the collection. We photograph everything and keep notebooks.

How do you produce your first samples?

All samples are made in the studio, and if I am traveling, the team will send images of development samples by phone.

What do you define as a range within a collection?

Little families. I use a range grid, which gives me an overview: for example, 70 percent dresses, 10 percent coats, 10 percent skirts, and 10 percent tops.

How much do your dresses sell for?

They start at £600 ($950) and go up to £2,000 ($3,200) in the department stores. Everything we show is for sale. A special one-off gown sold in Barneys or La Moda can go for £30,000 ($48,000).

How many looks do you show?

About forty-two, with the first ten looks setting the feel of the show.

Do you collaborate with anyone else?

Yes, Stephen Jones for the hats, Christian Louboutin for shoes. Also LCF, Swarovski, and MAC are sponsors. I also work with Dell Intel, LG Phones, Tanqueray No. Ten, and CPL perfumes.

Do you work with a stylist?

Yes, Katie Grand. We have meetings throughout the season and finalize colors and fabrics together.

Where do you sell your collection?

We have a showroom in Paris to show to store directors and head buyers for two weeks after the shows.

10 Giles Deacon, A/W 2014.

10

SIBLING
Joe Bates, Sid Bryan,
and Cozette McCreery

How do you start your collections?

We always start with a group brainstorming session, discussing themes or specific ideas that are interesting to us. We do not work to trends or market movements; instead we rely on our own instincts. We discuss images we have collated or found garments we may have gathered.

Are your collections seasonal?

Very much so: as we are knit-specific, it is very important to create pieces that are still desirable in summer, which is a challenge. Knit is synonymous with winter and warmth, so producing garments that have the correct feel for summer is very specific—yarn selection is key to this.

How do you compile a color palette and motifs?

Vibrant color is part of our initial brainstorming, which will raise questions and ideas for further development and research. We won the first Dulux Color Award and Best Use of Color in Fashion & Beauty. This will be readdressed later in the process when the collection has taken form, to ensure cohesion as a range. Our knit house signatures include leopard

motifs, skulls, skeletons, monsters, tattoos, slogans, and Breton stripes. SISTER by Sibling offers the same integrity and spirit for women.

Where do you source your yarns?

Our yarns are sourced worldwide: Scotland, Italy, and the Far East. We have established relationships with many yarn agents, and we visit Pitti Filati, a yarn trade fair in Italy.

How do you develop your shapes and silhouettes?

It is important for us to question traditional shape and form with knit. This has two very contrasting outcomes for us: one is our drive to create new and abstracted forms, challenging what is expected of both a knitwear shape and a menswear form. The other is our joy in creating knitted reproductions of recognized design classics, such as the trench coat, leather motorcycle jacket, [and] boating blazer; feats of engineering that are correct to the smallest detail.

How many are in your team?

Our team has a core of six, but this will swell at peak times to about twelve. We have people with a great variety of skills: hand knitters, machine knitters, pattern cutters, and embroiderers.

Where and how do you create your first samples?

Our studio is a fully functioning knit atelier. We have a wide variety of industrial machinery to allow us to create a great number of our first samples in-house. This allows us to experiment very much more than most companies. We will simultaneously create knit swatches, experimenting with stitch and yarn, and toile the form for fit and proportion. Knit is very different to working in wovens because every garment or design starts with a yarn. We have to build our cloth from scratch for every single piece. This creates both great opportunities and problems.

Where do you show and sell your collections?

We have a showroom in Paris during Menswear Fashion Week, where we invite press and buyers to view the collection. Also we show during London Fashion Week within MAN. Awards so far are Newgen Men and Women, Fashion Forward for Menswear. We are also representing Europe in the Woolmark Prize.

How many looks do you have in your collection?

We try to keep to around fifteen pieces. That includes garments that are to appeal specifically to press rather than sales.

Do you work with a stylist and have PR?

We employ a stylist and a groomer for every shoot we produce. It is important for us to consider other professionals' opinions and artistic vision whenever presenting our work. Our PR is all kept in-house. This is vital to us, as it allows us to be guarded as to whom we allow to use our product and in what environment. This is necessary to keep our identity clear and consistent.

Do you consider sustainability when producing your collections?

It is a consideration, and we will always go for a more sustainable option given a choice. Ethical treatment of people and manpower is something we are very actively conscious of.

Interview: Sibling

COLIN MCNAIR,
Menswear Designer at John Varvatos

How do you start your collections?

We start with the color palette and then usually go to vintage appointments in London, Paris, and New York and collect new pieces we like. This kicks off a mood, feeling, or look, along with what John Varvatos himself is thinking and his direction. We will also be reading magazines for looks, proportions, and ideas; we try to visualize what we want to achieve. We will look at vintage patterns for shirt and tie layouts, knit and sweater swatch suppliers for stitches and patterns. Along with this, we will start to look at fabrics for all categories, at fabric fairs and suppliers we work with each season. We will discuss as teams what we are thinking and bounce ideas off each other. Based on all the above, I will also start to play with graphic ideas for T-shirts and begin working with graphic designers. We also look at past seasons and build SKU [stock-keeping unit] plans in terms of how much we developed last season and what was actually sold. We have meetings with sales teams to discuss good sellers and bad sellers, meet with retail stores to get feedback, and talk to customers.

How many collections do you design?

We design four collections a year: resort, spring, pre-fall, and fall. Each collection is approximately 120 pieces, which does not include all the colorways and different fabrications we offer. It's big!

How many are in the design team?

There's John (CEO of the company), who is heavily involved in design. I have four designers for the younger line: one for wovens (outerwear, jackets, shirts, pants); one for denim and casual; one for knits and sweaters; and an assistant. I oversee a team of technical designers who work on specifications and fitting, commenting through development and production stages. I also work with one graphic designer. The main collection line has four designers on wovens, three designers on knits and sweaters, and one for accessories. They are also supported by technical design.

Do you compile a color palette and, if so, how?

This is the first thing we do. We collect colors I like and images of color and start putting them together in a way that fits with season and inspiration. We have a color library of old fabric swatches, pantones, and yarns that we pull from.

How and where do you source fabrics?

Fabric/yarn fairs, such as Milano Unica, Première Vision, and Pitti Filati, and trips to Asia and Europe where we visit mills and look at their collections (we also have the mills visit us in the office). We mainly use fabrics from Asia (China, Korea, and Japan) and Italy.

Do you commission textiles: knit, print, weave, and embroidery?

We don't commission as such. We buy vintage shirtings from vintage suppliers and put them into work with our weavers and printers. I buy sweater stitches and patterns from knit designers.

How do you develop your shapes and silhouettes: flat pattern, draping, modeling on the stand?

We design the clothes and send out technical packs to factories to follow for making the first prototype. Technical packs consist of all designs, detail sketches, specs, materials, and all the information a factory needs to construct a garment. We usually have old styles to refer to for fit, on which we base new styles. If it's a new factory or a new fit, we usually try to send an example from past seasons or a vintage garment to copy.

Where and how do you create your first samples?

First samples are made from the tech packs we send out. We then get a first prototype back and fit/comment on it. We send these comments back to the factory, and they proceed to make a sample in the correct fabric with all the correct trim, wash, and finishing. If we are on time or we feel we need to see it again, we make a second prototype before making the actual sample.

Approximately how many are made for each collection?

A lot! The first stage is the most experimental, so we put a lot of work into this to see what looks best. We cancel things when we see them if they don't look good, and that's generally how we edit down to what we sample/show to buyers.

What do you define as a collection or a range?

A group of clothes that can consist of different categories, such as outerwear, leather, pants, jackets, denim (jeans), shirts, knits, sweaters, and accessories.

How many pieces on average per collection are for catwalk only?

None: the catwalk is taken directly from the designed collection.

How many pieces or exits are in each collection and does this vary by season or line?

Yes, it varies. I find the more focused and edited the collection, the better it sells. We usually develop and sample the collection, which is then edited by sales by 30 percent. They sell the edited selection and then usually find the collection is edited by a further 20 percent, as some things don't sell. We cannot predict what buyers will buy, and you have to offer a selection.

How do you present the collections to your clients?

The sales team sells the collections from our showrooms, which are in-house also.

How do you work with stylists, marketing, and PR for selling the collection?

Stylists work with John to style the show. After the show, the collections will be sold by the sales team and after selling season, the collections then go to PR who send out to magazines, photo shoots, and clients for selling and promotions.

Interview: Colin McNair

GORDON RICHARDSON,
Creative Director at Topman

Do you commission textiles?

Where there's a particular theme that requires specific textiles or techniques we rely on a small group of freelance practitioners to produce individual items. We have in-house graphic designers for all our prints development requirements.

How do you start your collections?

Topman Design is an in-house team effort. The team works on everything collectively, working around a theme that evolves and expands as we work into the nuances and detail of each collection. For example, the Spring/Summer '09 collection was based on two mavericks: Jean Prouvé, an architect who pioneered the use of steel in furniture design, and Graeme Obree, who built the first Olympic bike. For Autumn/Winter '13 we were inspired by an early pioneer who absorbs different cultures as he undertakes his exploits through life.

How do you develop your shapes and silhouettes?

We often use vintage finds that the team [has] sourced to form the basis of key silhouettes for Topman Design, where we like to juxtapose different shapes to create exciting yet subtle new proportions and silhouettes.

How many collections do you design?

Two main collections for Topman Design: Autumn/Winter and Spring/Summer shown on the catwalk at London Collections: Men and continuous mini collections for Topman main range based on trends and ongoing sales analysis.

Where and how do you create your first samples?

We send a block, finished pattern, and toile with specifications to our key suppliers in the Far East, who will produce the samples. We usually sample multiples of what we need for the show.

How and where do you source fabrics?

Fabrics for Topman Design are selected and sourced depending on the theme we are pursuing at the time. Main range fabrics are sourced globally.

What do you define as a collection or range?

A collection is an edited, focused point of view and has a "strong identifiable character." A range is broader and less specific, with wider appeal. Specific product ranges go across many different categories, which individual designers work on separately using previous seasons' sales information and trend influences discussed as a team.

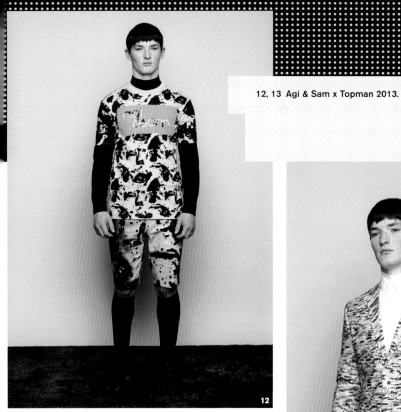

12, 13 Agi & Sam x Topman 2013.

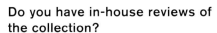

Do you have in-house reviews of the collection?

I will oversee the process from the beginning with the head of design until we feel we have a strong theme and direction, at which point we work closely with a recognized stylist to help structure and focus the collection so that it has a strong character and succinct viewpoint.

How do you show the collection?

We show on a catwalk as a part of London Collections: Men. We also continue to sponsor established and emerging talent through our Newgen Men and MAN initiatives.

Interview: Gordon Richardson

Interview

JOHN MOONEY,
Head of Menswear Design at ASOS

Where did you study?
I did my BA Fashion and Textiles at John Moores in Liverpool and did a placement at Littlewoods and then MA Womenswear at the RCA [Royal College of Art].

What did you do when you graduated?
I was interviewed for an internship at McQueen after my final show, which was tailored, traditional, and androgynous. I started in womenswear on a Monday working for Sarah Burton and by Wednesday was working on the first menswear collection. I stayed a year doing everything for the menswear collection and was then approached by Russell Fish at Littlewoods, who I met as a student, to join Topman, where I stayed six years before joining ASOS.

How many collections do you design for ASOS menswear?
ASOS Black is the only collection designed through outfits, whereas all other collections are ranges designed by product category. Categories led by experts in their field

include smart shirts and ties, casual shirts, outerwear, tailoring, shorts and swims, denim, footwear, underwear, loungewear, socks, and accessories covering 500 styles per category.

How many people in your team?
Sixteen designers, one per product area, and two graphic designers; within the design team structure there are senior designers, established designers, designers, and junior designers who work with four buyers each.

How do you start your collections/ranges?
Working with PR and the content team themes are established (e.g., skinny jeans), which are featured by the editorial team. ASOS menswear incorporates 6,500 styles in total. The width of the range will be agreed, including how many colorways per range.

How do you source your fabrics?
The team visits PV, Denim PV, and Texworld in Paris. We will follow PV trends and buy premier fabrics for ASOS Black, including Japanese denim and Harris tweed for the "Crafted In" range.

How are samples produced?

Design is all in-house, [where] freelance pattern cutters create initial patterns over a two-week period and technologists work on new styles without a block. They will work on global body shapes with sizes from XXX small to XXX large. Samples are made in the sample rooms within the factories.

How do you present your collection?

Products are signed off by phase (i.e., Autumn Phase 1, Winter Phase 2). The design team presents lookbooks and samples in the showroom in April, for a season launch in June, and seven global press looks for New York, Sydney, Shanghai, Moscow, Milan, Madrid, Paris, and London. The buying team, design team, and e-commerce production team collaborate on shoots for external and internal magazine using the in-house model agency.

What is the company message?

Keep it fresh, no hard push or selling but informing followers through social media and free magazine with a larger distribution than Grazia. ASOS is not just a shop but a fashion destination, offering newness all the time, including vintage, premium brands marketed through behind-the-scenes information and new style tips.

14 ASOS S/S 2014 press day.

Interview: John Mooney

14

Specialist collections

Specialist collections such as childrenswear, sportswear, knitwear and accessories cater for niche markets while also supporting a designer's larger mainstream collections. Most designers and producers who specialize in specific fashion product areas ensure that their collections are created and developed to work with seasonal design trends and directions—or at least acknowledge and complement them.

Footwear and accessories can create strong fashion trends and influences in their own right. They can be used to style the most basic items of clothing and update a fashion look. Many established companies rely on sales of footwear, bags, accessories, and licensed lines to maintain their businesses. Other specialist collections, such as childrenswear and sportswear, are typically created or commissioned around specific considerations and situations.

This chapter explores the development of collections within several different specialist areas.

1   Balenciaga, A/W 2014.

CHILDRENSWEAR

Trends within the area of children's fashion are subtle, but color, shape, and thematic influences combine to create a niche fashion movement that often reflects mainstream design in fashion and beyond. This is a continually growing market, with the current tendency for consumers to buy new rather than hand-me-down, although the sustainability agenda may change this.

Although loosely following fashion trends and the main fashion calendar, the childrenswear trade show cycle is different, and development of a childrenswear collection reflects more the age of the child, market level, and type of clothing—formal or casual. The design and development processes are similar to other fashion product areas in terms of fabric, color and shape development, sampling, and manufacturing. As is common in womenswear and menswear, each designer and retailer has individual sizing and labeling specifics, which are devised and monitored within individual businesses.

Childrenswear is an area of the fashion industry that is often overlooked by students when considering a career, but with most fashion students concentrating on womenswear or menswear, there are potentially more job opportunities within this specialist market.

Designer

Many international designers extend their collections from womenswear or menswear into childrenswear, such as Baby Dior, Armani Junior, Moschino Kids, Ralph Lauren, and Gucci. Stella McCartney and Roksanda Ilincic launched childrenswear collections after having children themselves. Burberry and Paul Smith also include childrenswear as a main part of their collections and campaigns. Markus Lupfer has launched Designers for Debenhams's first childrenswear range with celebrity Donna Air, including his signature sequined characters seen in his womenswear collections.

CHARACTER MERCHANDISE

The use of licensed characters as cartoon images on childrenswear is now mainstream, especially in the mass-market and in particular nightwear. In 2013, Riccardo Tisci launched the "Bambi" sweatshirt on the catwalk at Givenchy, displaying a reversal of the trend for childrenswear to be influenced by womenswear.

High street

The high street has entered the childrenswear market successfully by offering mini versions of their adult ranges, as seen at Gap Kids first followed by Zara Kids, H&M, and Monsoon. Old Navy in the United States focuses on family, including teen and kids collections with strong graphics and color in their seasonal offerings.

Designing for children

The childrenswear market has its own exhibition, Pitti Bimbo, twice a year in Florence, where established Italian childrenswear brand Chicco have an impressive stand. This is a major influence for mass-market childrenswear in chain stores, such as Marks and Spencer. With the emergence of supermarkets offering childrenswear—including schoolwear—at cut prices, more parents are buying clothing with their weekly groceries rather than going to specialist childrenswear boutiques.

Safety considerations

Although the research and design process for childrenswear is similar to adult wear, there are additional constraints. The childrenswear market is strictly controlled by health and safety legislation, related to fabric compositions, flammability, toxicity, and fastening security. Fabrics need to have a comfort factor, and fastenings and openings must be easy to negotiate so that children can dress and undress themselves. Necklines are larger in proportion to adult clothing, due to the size of children's heads in relation to the body. As with nightwear, fabrics for childrenswear will have stricter regulations on flammability and likewise dyes and printing inks need to be safe and sustainable.

Machine knitting is produced in one of two ways: flat-bed knitting creates flat fabric, which will be transformed into garments through cut and sew techniques; fully fashioned knitting creates garments that are shaped on the machine. Flat-bed knitting includes the high-end, labor-intensive intarsia knitting, where yarns are laid in the courses of weft knitting to form irregular, one-off patterns and motifs. Digital knitwear technology developed by the Japanese manufacturer Shima Seiki has enabled whole garment knitwear to be produced. Traditionally knitwear is knitted in parts—front, back, sleeves—and assembled by linking or overlocking afterward. Wholegarment knitting is a Shima patented laborsaving brand, has no seams, and is completely reversible.

Most fashion knitwear is weft-knitted; however, in the 1950s Ottavio and Rosita Missoni in Northern Italy developed colorful patterned artisanal knitwear collections using warp knitting, which is a cross between knitting and weaving. While Missoni reigned in Milan, another iconic knitwear designer, Sonia Rykiel, was establishing herself in Paris. Rykiel was known as the Queen of Knitwear in the United States and demonstrated "what you can do with a bit of yarn." Her collections were based on novelty and slogan sweaters, with her signature colorful stripes, classic nautical references, and "boy sweaters."

2 Cara Delevingne modeling for Sister by Sibling, A/W 2013.

2

In the 1970s, Scottish Designer Bill Gibb was inspired by traditional craft and ethnic cultures. Together with his partner, Kaffe Fassett, he designed some of the most exciting knitwear collections of the decade. Their use of vibrant colors, organic motifs, and extravagant layering of knit was influential in the development of fashion knitwear. Gibb went on to collaborate with Missoni, stating at the time, "What women want to wear in the daytime is beautiful knits."

In the 1990s, Japanese designer Issey Miyake used new technology to create integral warp knitting, launching his iconic "a-poc" collection, which literally means "a piece of cloth." This new concept required the customer to cut up the synthetic knitted cloth, with its computer-generated print, and produce tubular garments that could be worn in a multiple of ways. This innovative process resulted in a capsule collection of a dress, skirt, underwear, hat, gloves, socks, and a bag, all cut from one piece of cloth.

Designers and brands

Knitwear collections have now come full circle, with designers revisiting traditional handcraft techniques. The value of the heritage of hand knits from the island communities on Arran, Jersey, and Guernsey are often used as references for fashion collections. Designers will also commission knits from specialists in the same way that they do prints. Scottish heritage brand Pringle of Scotland, known for its technical innovation and argyle pattern, have employed designers Clare Waight Keller and Alistair Carr to design collections for the catwalk. The use of clashing colorful hand knitting and crochet for a total catwalk collection was first seen at Clare Tough's MA graduate collection at Central Saint Martins. Sibling has experimented with giant crochet pieces in their collections for men and the womenswear line Sister.

CAMPAIGN FOR WOOL

The campaign was launched in 2010 to bring awareness to the properties of wool as a unique, natural, renewable, and biodegradable fabric on a global scale. It brings together wool producers, knitwear designers, artisans, and manufacturers with a common aim. The campaign has also launched the Wool School where universities were partnered with high-street retailers Topshop, Hobbs, Whistles, and Harvey Nichols to produce capsule ranges to promote wool.

YARNS

The advanced technology of today's machines means that one-piece, seamless garments can be produced as well as garments in the finest of yarns on fine gauge (the gauge is the number of needles per inch—sixteen or twelve for fine gauge). Traditionally yarns are made from natural fibers, such as lambs' wool, cashmere, cotton, silk, and wool. Modern yarns are being continuously developed and improved: synthetic fibers, such as polyamide, polyester, microfiber, and spandex are all used to create high-performance knitted fabrics. The newest wool from the arrest of sheep has been used to create an exclusive fine-gauge yarn.

3   Charli Cohen, A/W 2013.

3

ACTIVE SPORTSWEAR

Active sportswear is influenced as much by fashion as performance. Technical fabrics and digital processes for manufacturing are the key to the development of the collection.

In the early 1980s, American designer Norma Kamali launched a fashion business celebrating the use of traditional sweatshirting as a fashion fabric. This proved successful at a time when exercise and healthier lifestyles were beginning to dictate a new style of clothing. Kamali recently revisited this type of fashion by collaborating with Everlast in the United States to design an extensive range of fashion sweats for today's body-conscious woman. Around the same time in London, two British designers launched their Bodymap label, which was a reductive, loose style based on Californian sportswear.

The sports world has inspired a number of fabric and garment developments specific to athletic performance and associated activities. The international interest, appeal, and support for modern sport has proven irresistible to designers and producers. Companies have been swift to collaborate with a number of fashion and product designers to raise consumers' awareness of sportswear as a credible lifestyle fashion statement. Sportswear brand Puma has collaborated with conceptual designer Hussein Chalayan. The Fred Perry label has worked with Comme des Garçons in refreshing the iconic sports polo shirt, and designer Felipe Oliveira Baptista has been appointed Head Designer at Lacoste. Adidas has successfully created Y3 with Yohji Yamamoto, to include full catwalk presentation of this sportswear and fashion fusion. Stella McCartney has also consulted for Adidas and was the designer of the official Olympics uniform for the London Olympics 2012.

CORPORATE WEAR

Corporate wear is designed to portray a company's image, brand values, and in most examples, brand identity. Issues related to health and safety, wearability, durability, and care are all factors that inform the final range of garments. Considerations must also allow for the wide range of wearers—body sizing, working environments, religious dress requirements, and even personalization limitations. Color, prints, and logos are aligned to the company's branding in order to promote a unified, professional image.

Banks, hotels, restaurants, retailers, and service providers have adopted the approach that employees should represent the company and its mission statement values when dealing with customers. More and more organizations are adding value to the customer experience by employing recognized fashion designers to create corporate fashion collections.

Perhaps the largest corporate investment in fashion, with international recognition, is the uniform worn by national airlines. These garments take years to develop, trial, amend, and produce. The range of separates must be suitable for the tasks required of each wearer, while conveying professionalism and a dependable authority. Many ranges must also have a fashion lifespan of up to ten years, which presents huge challenges for the designer.

Many airlines are keen to employ internationally recognized designers, and as such, the garments have become iconic over the years. Braniff International in the United States famously employed Emilio Pucci as part of its entire corporate makeover in the late 1960s. The garments were unlike anything seen before or since; futuristic and colorful, they were as close to fashion as corporate clothing can get. In the 1970s, Braniff commissioned Halston to dress its cabin crews. John Rocha and Vivienne

Westwood have both designed for Virgin Atlantic, Ferré for Korean Air, Balmain for Singapore Airlines, YSL for Qantas, Julien MacDonald for British Airways, Dior and Calvin Klein for Scandinavian Airlines, Armani for Alitalia, and Kate Spade for Song. Renowned for the most chic flight attendants, Air France's cabin crews are currently dressed by Christian Lacroix. By aligning themselves with international, premium fashion brands, these airlines are communicating corporate values to customers, as well as adding to the travel experience.

Field Grey, a small design company in London, offers a design service for uniforms as diverse as Yotel hotels, Nude Skincare, and Vertu mobile phones. As well as practicality, brand value and customer care are key factors when designing for corporate clients.

4   **Tom's Kitchen. Bespoke dyed duck cotton workwear aprons by Field Grey.**

5 An iconic shoe sketch by Nicholas Kirkwood.

5

FOOTWEAR, BAGS, AND ACCESSORIES

Collections of footwear and accessories, such as leather bags, can be created as individual fashion statements or may be commissioned by a designer as a part of a complete fashion look. It would be impossible to ignore the recent growth and interest within this fashion area and its influence on consumers' choices.

Many of the processes used in production still rely on handcraft skills and many years' experience to achieve the highest quality standards. Footwear in the middle and mass-markets is mostly produced in Brazil, China, and Portugal. Footwear made in Italy and Spain is more expensive and is therefore found in more upmarket brands. Sneakers and sports shoes are mainly produced in Thailand, China, and Vietnam, where significant investment has created a profitable, quality-secured industry. Mass production of footwear has disappeared in the UK, mainly due to labor costs, market changes, and competition from other areas of the world. As such, the materials and methods used to create leather accessories and footwear are unique to this product area.

Twice each year, Linea Pelle in Bologna showcases trends and developments in leather and leather products. Around 1,300 exhibitors from approximately forty-five countries attend this trade exhibition. Exhibitors include tanneries, designers, and accessory/component manufacturers. Visiting professionals can find information on related trends and innovations in technology and materials. This is the starting point for many footwear designers.

The next stage is to design the fashion shapes for the new collection. A *last* forms the basis of the shoe, and it will dictate the toe shape, heel height, and variations on the foot coverage for each style. As for clothing, patterns are cut and then checked against the last. Heels (especially high heels) may be carved or created separately, as these often become embellishments or features of the finished shoes.

Lasts were traditionally carved from wood. At the very top end of the footwear market, companies such as Ferragamo, would create personalized lasts for special customers, made to individual specification. Today, rapid prototype technology can create exact requirements for lasts; this is both faster and cheaper than before, thereby adding to the designer's scope for innovation and quick response.

Footwear designers, such as Christian Louboutin, Manolo Blahnik, Georgina Goodman, Charlotte Olympia, and Nicholas Kirkwood, create beautiful, desirable shoes. They design special collections in collaboration with fashion designers along with their own ranges. Many of these shoes are produced to the equivalent standards of haute couture clothing: they are expensive, collectable, and treasured by consumers across the world. Recent collaborations include iconic British/Japanese print design duo Eley Kishimoto who collaborated with heritage brand Clarks shoes, using their archive flash print on desert boots for their Spring/Summer 2013 installation at LFW. Phoebe Philo also launched printed skater shoes with thicker soles, costing ten times the price of the original Vans skateboard shoe, for her Autumn/Winter 2013 collection for Celine.

Like fashion clothing, soft leather bags and accessories are created by cutting pattern pieces to be stitched or glued into shape. The color, finish, and leather craft techniques, such as carving, brogue work, burnishing, and spraying, can all alter and enhance the surface of many natural skins. Stitching, printing, embroidery, and the availability of fixtures, fastenings, and strengthening (known as *furniture* or *hardware*) enable endless design possibilities.

Bags and leather goods are usually developed by an accessories designer or team, following the direction set by the fashion clothing—to include color, shape, silhouette, surface embellishments, handles, fastenings, and treatments. Each item is created in the same way as garments, in that patterns are created and samples are made for approval. Unlike clothing, however, the patterns have to fit the skins; wastage can be high, depending on the type of skin and size of the pattern pieces, and taking into account any natural flaws and imperfections.

SPECIALIST COURSES

UK courses in footwear and accessories are offered at London College of Fashion (Cordwainers) and De Montford University, Leicester.

Footwear, bags, and accessories

Interview

EVA KARAYIANNIS,
Owner of Caramel
Baby & Child

How and when did you start your company?

I've always loved children's clothes and used to collect them, even before I had my own [children]. After my daughters were born, I was dissatisfied with what was out there and was encouraged by a friend who was in fashion, and Caramel Baby & Child began in 1999. I started by selling handcrafted knitwear from Peru, and beautiful clothes by small designers from London and the Cotswolds. Not long after, I started designing my own collections. I had quite a clear idea of what I wanted my collection to be, and I think this was the reason people liked it. It was new and fresh and the timing was right.

How do you start developing a new collection?

I am always hungry and curious for each new inspiration, and over the years I have really learned to "exercise my eyes." Everything has the potential to be used as inspiration for future collections—the pattern of shadows on a wall, a piece of exquisite tile work, the way a skirt moves as a child runs. When I see something that captures my attention, I take a photo on my iPhone, tear the image out of the magazine or save it to my computer, and in this way, I build an archive of inspiration that I refer to as I start development. I pull out those images that are speaking to me most

at the time, and these will form the basis, with fabrics and color references being added to build a full picture.

How many do you have in your team?

I head up our in-house design team of five, working on knitwear, wovens, and production. Each season, we also use pattern cutters and print designers. At head office, we also have our web, marketing, wholesale, retail, and logistics teams, as well as our sales teams that work in the stores. We have between thirty-five to forty people employed across the business.

Where do you source your sample and production fabrics?

Along with visiting the usual large tradeshows, such as Première Vision and Milano Unica, I look to vintage when developing fabrics, and so I find a lot in various vintage stores and fairs. We will then recolor and rework them for our collections.

Specialist collections

6, 7 Caramel Baby &
       Child, A/W 2013.

6

7

Interview: Eva Karayiannis

8 Caramel, S/S 2014 fabric board.

How do you compile your color palette?

In order for a collection to be exciting, I choose colors that are in harmony with one another and then add in a color that's totally "wrong"; that's what makes it contemporary. Each year, I'm instinctively attracted to certain colors—I prefer one over another, or am particularly drawn to a certain color combination—and there is not a clear reason why, they just feel right. It might be a porcelain cup or some paper from Japan that's the perfect shade of cream; again it's all about exercising your eye.

Do you work with print designers?

I love print and feel it is integral to our business. It sits beautifully with childrenswear and is a really nice way to express the essence of a collection. I want each of my collections to have a strong personality and as it is hard to buy this, we develop our own prints. I get a lot of inspiration from fabrics and porcelain, and then we play with color, pairing soft and hard, sweet yet confident. I enjoy working with print

designers and have worked with the same ones for many years. They know Caramel, and we have created a bond.

Do you work with embroidery companies?

We do work with embroidery companies but we develop our own embroideries and rework them to sit alongside our prints. In fact we have transferred the prints to embroidery many times. Again, I will often look to vintage for my inspiration.

How do you create your silhouettes and patterns?

I find it exciting developing silhouettes for children; there are so many factors that you have to take into consideration. You want to create something new, exciting, and different, but you have to remember that you are creating for a child. We stick to simple silhouettes and then add small details or play with proportions—a large collar for example—and in this way it becomes contemporary.

There are vintage references, but these are subtle. What's great about childrenswear is that up to a certain age you can consider children unisex; you can bring details and silhouettes from both womenswear and menswear. These details are what make good design. I don't overdesign or overembellish; that's not what Caramel is about.

Where do you produce your collections?

We want to use the best factories for our collections, and no one country does everything best. As long as the factory provides an ethical experience and produces for like-minded brands, then we want go to the one that is best for each individual technique. For example, we use the Far East for knitwear, a factory in Peru for our hand knits, and one in Madagascar for embroidery.

Where do you sell your collections?

We are an international brand that retails in our own monobrand stores in London, New York, Japan, and Singapore and online through our Web store, plus concessions in Selfridges and Fenwick. We wholesale our collection to over 100 independent retailers in more than fifteen countries, including key department stores, such as Le Bon Marché, Isetan, Barneys, and Luisa Via Roma.

How do you promote the collections?

We don't have a massive marketing budget and view our stores and Web site as key windows to our brand, connecting with customers face-to-face and digitally (via e-mail mailers and social media). Tradeshows, such as Pitti Bimbo and Playtime Paris, are important for promoting our collection to wholesale clients, and we produce digital and print lookbooks per season, shooting editorial images for use on our Web site and for press. We work with outside agencies, such as PR or web marketing, who provide support for our in-house teams.

Do you consult for other brands other than your own?

No.

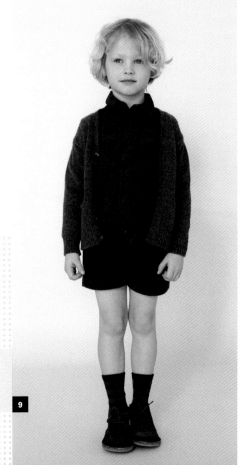

9   Caramel, A/W 2013.

9

Interview: Eva Karayiannis

Interview

SAM LEUTTON,
Cofounder and Codesigner
(with Jenny Postle) of Leutton Postle

Where did you study?
Central Saint Martins for Foundation,
BA and MA.

How and when did you and your partner start your company?
We started when I graduated my MA in 2011.
The timing was right, and I have no idea how anyone does this on their own.

How many do you have in your team?
Three.

How do you begin a new collection?
Research, research, research! Textiles usually always comes first for us, too.

Where do you source your sample yarns?
All over. We like to use some unusual stuff, so it can be from an Italian mill or something weird from a northern knitting shop.

How do you compile your color palette?
We're pretty free and easy with our colors, so we just keep going until we see what sticks.

Where do you produce your collection?
London.

What kind of knitting do you specialize in?
All kinds but mostly techniques that allow pattern. We used to do a lot of e-wrapping, but now it's a lot more intarsia and jacquard.

How do you create your silhouettes and patterns?
Just researching and toiling. We keep going and trying things on until we get somewhere that we're happy with.

Where do you produce your collections?
London.

Where do you sell your collections?
H. Lorenzo, LA; Primitive and Machine-A in London; and Avenue 32 online.

How do you promote the collections?
Using a mix of our Web site and social media.

Do you consult for other brands other than your own?
We are beginning to!

10, 11   Leutton Postle, A/W 2014.

Interview

CHARLI COHEN,
Sportswear Designer

Where and what did you study?
Fashion BA (Hons)—Kingston University.

How and when did you start your company?
I'd always planned to start my own brand as soon as I graduated. I created and integrated the Charli Cohen brand identity as part of my final BA collection, and Graduate Fashion Week provided me with an important launch pad. A few months later I was selected as a finalist for the WGSN Global Fashion Awards and subsequently received part sponsorship from Invista (creators of Lycra). This provided both the additional financial support and confidence in my business idea to move forward quickly. After a year of sourcing, setup, and careful planning, I launched my first collection for Spring/Summer '14.

How many collections do you produce a year?
Two.

How many looks do you show in each collection?
Fifteen to eighteen.

How do you start developing a new collection?
I plan the types of garments the range needs to include and roughly how these should come together into looks. This helps me keep the collection concise and edited as I move through the design process.

Where do you get your inspiration?
I start with primary research. This is often watching, photographing, and videoing different sports, disciplines, and the environment and surroundings these are done in. I'll usually find a detail or a shape early on that I get excited about. This then becomes a consistent design element or theme throughout the new collection.

How do you compile your color palette?
Usually, I have an idea of palette from my primary research; then I adapt this to what's available from the mills for the season. However, the fabrics in themselves are inspiring, so it may be that I find a certain color or texture and decide to work the palette around that because I *have* to have it in the collection.

12   Charli Cohen, A/W 2013.

12

Where do you produce your collections?

England.

Where do you sell your collections?

As a wholesaler, I do a lot of direct communicating with buyers and also have a presence at major shows, such as London Fashion Week and Who's Next Paris. I also retail via pop-ups and trunk shows.

How do you promote the collections?

Through both traditional media and digital/social media—my promotion is entirely through PR campaigns, with no paid advertising.

Where do you make your samples?

At the same UK factory I work with for my production.

Do you work with print designers or other specialists?

No.

How do you create your silhouettes and patterns?

Designing performance wear, I need to ensure everything supports and moves with the body correctly, so I watch people train and establish the needs and potential problems with a certain garment. The ergonomics and seam placement required will tend to inform the silhouette. Draping doesn't really work for this, so I start with high-spec 2D designs and then work with my factory to sample and performance test toiles until the 3D looks and functions the way I want it to.

Are you sponsored by another company?

I received part sponsorship from Invista for my first and second collections but am primarily self-funded.

Do you design for other brands other than your own?

I've done various short-term freelance projects alongside designing for Charli Cohen.

Where do you source your production fabrics?

I source both my sampling and production fabrics from Italy. The Invista sponsorship opened up a lot of doors for me with sourcing and I was fortunate to have my pick of mills.

Interview: Charli Cohen

Interview

TRACY MULLIGAN,
Head of Design at
People Tree

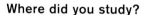

Where did you study?
One year at Kingston, then two years at CSM for BA Fashion and Textiles.

What did you do when you graduated?
I interned at Daniel Hechter in Paris and then started my own business in 1992. I then formed a new company, Sonnentag Mulligan, in partnership with CSM graduate Barbara Sonnentag, and we secured M&S New Generation sponsorship of £25,000 per annum for three years. We were nominated for a British Fashion Award and showed on BFC [British Fashion Council] schedule at LFW. We sold our collections to Browns, Harvey Nichols, Harrods, Whistles, and Jones. I then went solo with Mulligan and did consultancy for French Connection.

Where did you sell your collection?
I showed off-schedule at the Metropolitan Hotel and sold to Colette in Paris, Liberty, Saks, and Barneys in New York.

How did you produce your collections?
At Sonnentag Mulligan, we produced at small, high-end CMT [cut, make, and trim] units in the Greater London area, where they were able to produce small dockets from 20 to 200 and above.

How did you become head of design at People Tree?
I was approached to work for People Tree in 2008. I had already started to read about the company and take interest in ethical clothing, as it was receiving a lot of press attention. Safia Minney MBE, the CEO and owner, contacted design recruitment agency Indesign, and I have been there six years.

What is People Tree's key identity?
People Tree sits in the upper high-street price point, along with stores such as Jigsaw and Toast. We are a small independent brand known for our nature-inspired prints and vintage styling. We create day-to-evening and casual wear, and our customer is thirty plus, professional, and socially aware. People Tree shows it is possible to create collections while respecting the people who make the garments, as well as the planet and animals.

Where do you source your fabrics?
We will go to PV to see the key colors and trends and eco developments in fabrics. We start to develop our fabrics three months before PV, as it is a long process. We use View by David Shah and Next Look to see what the key trends are and what will continue.

We cannot follow trends that are synthetic (e.g., shine) and would not use materials that are harmful to the planet and its resources.

We try to use, as much as possible, natural buttons, glass beads, and fabrics—all of which are recyclable or biodegradable and cause the least harm to the environment. This is a stark contrast to the current fashion industry today, where there is little consideration to dye effluent and fabric waste, et cetera. We spend a lot of time on checking our supply chain and ensuring that any component we use complies with the fair trade standards. We manufacture in India, where they produce machine woven 100 percent organic cotton in farming communities, which are processed in a mill using AZO-free dyes. We then go to Bangladesh, where hand skills include hand weaving, hand embroidery, and block printing.

How many collections do you design a year?
Two whole collections with two trends and one resort.

How do you compile your color palette?
We subscribe to Li Edelkoort's Trend Union and View on Color and select colors to reflect the seasonal drops, with fresh colors added in transitional drops.

How many people do you have in your team?
I work closely with two designers to create the fabrics, prints, and embroideries each season. We try to repeat some hand weaves, as these take a lot of development time for the producers. We are always considerate of the producers' time, and we try to avoid waste, so if a fabric design has not worked for one season, we try to use the next.

How does your team research a collection?
They start with mood or theme boards and look at Euro View for trend predictions.

For example our Spring/Summer theme, "Artisan," will have three trends that resonate with the People Tree brand. They will also refer to style.com and vogue.com to see high-end designer collections to analyze new trends. They will also continue with best sellers adapted for the following season.

How do you create your patterns?
We have a pattern cutter who will produce the sample pattern for the producers with a very detailed specification sheet. It can take four to six weeks for the producers to produce samples. Anything that is more complex will have a toile produced also.

How many samples do you produce, and how do you edit the collection?
The cutter will produce between thirty and fifty patterns for 150 samples per full collection. The collections are then edited down through two internal selection meetings. Some pieces are eliminated on price and others to balance the collection.

How do you sell the collection?
Our lookbook and catalogs are shot mainly by Safia Minney, our CEO and Founder. The wholesale team sells at our head office and at trade shows in [the] UK and Europe. We have agents in Ireland and Europe and select samples for different regions. We sell online on Atterly Road and ASOS and at high-end department stores, such as John Lewis, as well as cool, ethical independents, such as Mercantile in Spitalfields.

Who does People Tree collaborate with?
We work with high-end designers on mini collections to spread the fair trade message. We are currently working with Orla Kiely, Zandra Rhodes, Eley Kishimoto, Bora Aksu, Richard Nicoll, Peter Jensen, and Simeon Farrar. We are paid royalties for these collaborations.

Interview: Tracy Mulligan

NICHOLAS KIRKWOOD,
Shoe Designer

How do you start your collections?

Once production has finished, I wait for a gap of two weeks, then I buy a block of paper and with a 2D pencil, I draw base ideas continuously for the next collection. My aesthetic is the brand: architectural, feminine, masculine, extreme, and always high heels. I divide the seventeen or so styles into four sections based on my customers: leader, follower, exquisite, and intellectual.

What is the next process after drawing your designs?

I draw on the vacuum form prototype last to make the first pattern (instead of on masking tape on lasts, which is the traditional way). I then hand this over to a *modeliste* [pattern maker] in Italy. My shoes are high-end and handcrafted rather than computer generated.

Do you look at the work of other shoe designers at all?

Only to check that I am not doing the same designs. My new designs are usually a new interpretation on a few styles.

How many collections do you do in a year?

Two main collections: one for Spring/Summer and one for Autumn/Winter. I show in my studio during London Fashion Week in September and February, and I also show in Paris, Milan, and New York. Micam, a trade show in Milan, overlaps, and I invite press to a hotel there.

How many are in your design team?

Just me! Christopher, who works with me, covers sales, marketing, production, and suppliers. He will range plan and merchandise each group and is responsible for the twenty-nine or so samples I will produce in different fabrications within the seventeen styles in the collection.

Do you produce a color palette for each season?

I go to the leather fair at Linea Pelle in Bologna at the end of October and see ranges of colored leather. It is important to have color balance in the range; for example, last season I did black shoes with electric blue heels. I will usually choose four or five colors that sit well together. I can also dye small quantities for special colors.

How and where do you source your skins?

I use mainly leather and suede, and I also use satin, which is stiffened with backing cloth especially for shoes, all from Italy. Vintage shoes are often in kidskin, but I don't use it for collections as I like to use new-looking leathers and special skins, such as alligator.

Do you commission embroidery or other surface decoration?

I have worked with Swarovski to soften the hard architectural, angular lines, and this application will add delicacy to the shoe.

How do you work on your shapes?

Once I have the initial paper pattern from my drawing, I will refine and change it by maybe adding pleats or adding a platform heel. I can get a shoe sample made in two days from a new last shape and heel shape. For a new heel, I have an aluminum mold made in two sizes: 35 and 41. For production there will be four sizes of heels: 36, 37.5, 39, and 40.5. The samples are one-offs, and my shoes have hidden parts to hold the foot, disguised by a more extravagant outer part—similar in construction to architecture. Shapes are usually in stories of two.

Do you collaborate with other designers or companies?

I design shoes for Pellini, who also has Jonathan Saunders as a designer, and Alberta Ferretti in Italy, as well as my main line. I have also made shoes for Hardy Amies, Chloe, Boudicca, Gareth Pugh, Clare Tough, Basso & Brooke, and Zac Posen.

Do you have a PR company working for you?

Yes, I use Relative PR, who also represents Christopher Kane in London.

Interview: Nicholas Kirkwood

Interview

OLIVER RUUGER,
Luxury Accessories Designer
and Owner of Oliver Ruuger

Where and what did you study?
I studied BA Fashion at Kingston University
and MA Fashion Artefact at London College
of Fashion.

How and when did you start your company?
I started the company in April 2012 as a
result of finding the right people who believed
in the idea and were willing to commit their
time and energy full time to the cause.

How do you define your work?
Highly labor-intensive luxury fashion
objects, which border between sculpture
and product.

How do you start developing a new collection of pieces?
I do not plan for a collection at all at the
start, nor do I have a specific premeditated
method for approaching a project. It always
starts with an idea for an experiment with a
material or shape and evolves naturally from
there. Often it has been at the back of my
mind for a long time, sometimes years. I try
not to pre-analyze or set fixed concepts, as it
makes me feel too restricted. I believe in the
designer working intuitively.

Describe the crafts that you have specialized in.
Traditional leathercraft in conjunction with
digital subtractive and additive manufacturing
would be ones which the studio holds good
expertise about; however, we always like
to experiment with different crafts and
techniques across the board.

What equipment do you have in your studio?
In-house we work with full manufacturing
equipment for leathercraft, with some
specialized equipment for wood and
metalworking.

Where do you get your inspiration?
Mostly from mistakes and misunderstandings—
often the things that happen by chance or turn
out as they were not meant to give ideas one
cannot categorize nor reference—those are the
best kind of inspiration.

Do you still sketch ideas or do you work straight into 3D?
First 3D, then sketch to remember, visualize,
and communicate.

Where do you source your sampling leather and other materials?
I work directly with highly specialized
tanneries from all over the world.

13 Oliver Ruuger,
"The Possession."

13

Where do you make your first prototypes?

We make not only prototypes but also production and bespoke orders at the London studio.

Where do you sell your products?

Mostly directly to [the] customer, as well as to select stores in the UK, United States, Japan, and China.

How many pieces do you make for an order generally?

Most often it is a single piece for a customer or a small limited number for a high-end store.

Have you exhibited your work?

Yes, our pieces have been exhibited in various galleries and exhibitions such as "Added Value?"—a Crafts Council exhibition; "The Great Festival of Creativity" in Istanbul, Hong Kong, and Shanghai; The Zabludovicz Collection, MAXXI Museum of Modern Art in Rome, and others.

Do you design for other brands other than your own brand?

I consult as a creative director for an international accessories brand.

Do you have a PR or sales agent?

Yes, we have an in-house sales team.

14

14 Oliver Ruuger,
"Umbrella Apple."

Interview: Oliver Ruuger

The student collection

Studying in a fashion course offers you time to develop your imagination, improve your professional awareness, and respond to a series of challenges. A three- or four-year BA undergraduate Fashion Design course will cover essential skills and encourage creativity and experimentation through briefs that are challenging and current.

Initial first-year projects will focus on learning and applying creative, practical, and contextual skills within defined project briefs. These briefs may include designing and producing two- and three-dimensional ideas as an individual or within a team. The second year is usually industry focused, with either work placements or sponsored project competitions, which may lead to paid internships internationally. Companies sponsoring projects will brief students on key brand values, market level, and signature, and emphasize the parameters within a brand, season, customer, fabric type, or story. Additional factors, such as working with print, knit, or embroidery specialists, may contribute to some collections.

As a guide to the processes involved in the creation and realization of your final collection, the following activities represent the key stages of process. Be prepared to keep a cross-check between each stage, as you may need to go back to revisit an element of research or early development when reviewing your progress and considering the final presentation. There are no clear end points to each stage; even at the final presentation, there are elements that could be redeveloped or refined. This is symptomatic of fashion, where creativity is not just about problem solving but also producing a proposal or statement that should intrigue or connect with the onlooker. The most successful student collections tell a story; they embody a captivating narrative. The collection must communicate this without the visual research or written explanation. This chapter will help guide you as you develop your own final student collection.

1   Sophie Wetherell,
    Graduate Fashion
    Week, London.

THE BRIEF

This may be referred to as the final brief, proposal, statement of intent, or concept outline. Regardless of its name, the activity and process is the same. Begin by asking yourself what will showcase your skills and creativity in the best way. Some students approach this stage of their final collection with vague or unrealistic ideas, being driven to making the ultimate personal catwalk statement. Without reflection, research, and a great deal of hard work, this will not work. Creativity in fashion exists within a context—and for this final college collection, you create your own context, within your brief. On the following pages, we will discuss the considerations that should inform your brief and collection.

2, 3, 4 The brief. Stefanie Tschirky investigates the beauty of clean lines and geometric forms to challenge the prevailing silhouettes in fashion. Her work is often influenced by contemporary architecture and mathematical theories which results in her designs seeming to be dynamic structures between the built environment and the wearer.

movement,
space, volume
the layer between the body and the urban environment

movement,
space, volume
the layer between the body and the urban environment

3

movement,
space, volume
the layer between the body and the urban environment

4

The brief

5, 6 This project, by Alexandra Baldwin, responds to the FAD Competition title "Multisensory." Alexandra chose to look at Yves Klein's *The Void* work and his idea that blue is the most sensory color.

LOOK 1   LOOK 2

F.A.D **THE VOID**

5

Your skills

You should think hard about your particular strengths. For example, if your skills are in tailoring, draping, or creative cutting, then your designs should demonstrate and use this expertise. Or if your skills are in fabric development, print, weave, knit, or embroidered textiles, then use these specialist skills in your final collection. Experiment with fabric, color, shape, and detail to come up with something new or reworked from traditional pieces. Many designers will develop collections based on classic iconic garments, using menswear for womenswear, for example, or restyling the biker jacket or trench in unexpected fabrics. Examples of this include Sophie Hulme's sequined parka and Sibling's knitted trench.

Most employers are looking for graduates who are innovators but can also demonstrate an understanding of the stages of design through to realization. The presentation of your collection is important, but your portfolio, personal presentation, and depth of understanding will secure your first and subsequent jobs. Decide what this collection will say about your interests and your awareness of fashion.

Your customer

Consider defining your ideal customer. By imagining a customer, you can begin to create your own muse or inspiration. Where does your customer live, and what is in his or her wardrobe? Where do your customers shop, and how do they wear fashion to define themselves? Go and visit the shops you would identify as stockists for your collection, and look at the existing stock. Detail the prices and the finish on the garments and begin to inform yourself of the realities of market levels, visual merchandising, and how fashion communicates through branding and creative identity. How do clothes connect with customers at the point of retail? When we buy fashion, what stories do we tell about ourselves?

The student collection

Your competitors

Your competitors exist in every fashion area, market level, and retail possibility. Your work may be innovative, or redefine a particular area, technique, or product, but fashion is a discipline that exists in a wider context and constantly references itself—past and present. Even if you approach fashion as art rather than design, you will be able to find a range of practitioners and collaborators who have taken this view. Once you have a clear idea of your product and market type, then you should be able to identify the competition.

Quality, luxury, and rarity can be defined in any product, so once you know who your competitors are, study their products closely. There is no substitute for trying clothes on and seeing firsthand how the garment feels, examining the cut and stitching. Look, too, at details, such as buttons and the quality of any branding or labeling. At the other end of the scale, you should be prepared to look at

mass-market fashion, as ranges are often on-trend and produced to appeal to greater numbers of fashion consumers.

Remember, too, that your fellow graduates are your competitors. You could consider niche areas, such as plus-size fashion, swimwear, childrenswear, and evening wear, for example, which will provide you with a specific starting point. These can help position you for the future, as you will stand out from the hundreds of womenswear-related graduates who enter the job market each year, and increase your potential in securing employment. Most employers look for evidence of research, development, realization, and presentation within a portfolio.

These skills are easily showcased by collating your portfolio as a series of projects, to show diversity and competence across different ranges, market-based studies, and self-defined work—which is typically your final college project.

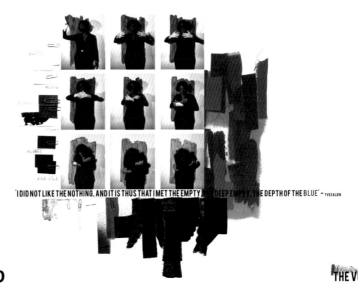

'I DID NOT LIKE THE NOTHING, AND IT IS THUS THAT I MET THE EMPTY, THE DEEP EMPTY, THE DEPTH OF THE BLUE' – YVES KLEIN

F A.D

THE VOID

The brief

6

Achieving your aspiration

If you realize that you will need assistance and input to produce your collection, you have the opportunity to build a team to make this happen—as most designers do. Time planning, delegation, and management of the project are part of the whole process. A good starting point is to have a draft collection plan (or line-up), where you can begin to deconstruct each piece into activities and deadlines. Use a calendar to plot key dates against the processes involved, which will help you to get organized and manage your schedule. Allow enough lead time to secure sponsorship for fabrics, trims, shoes, and so on. Remember also that most students will be thinking, writing, and developing ideas at the same time as you.

Cost

You should be realistic when planning and costing your collection. Fabrics, finish, and trims should reflect a realism within your chosen market or your target customer. Again, pay close attention to how clothes are cut and finished. If you are aiming for an upmarket collection, the typical retail price may be up to 300 percent of the wholesale price. If you have made any industry contacts as part of your study (work placements, sponsored projects, or visiting speakers from industry), then you should consider contacts as potential support or sponsors. Some student collections can cost huge amounts of money to produce, but this is not a prerequisite for success.

Fabrics, yarns, and trims

Buying fabrics in retail outlets should be your last resort. Visit trade fairs, such as Première Vision for fabrics, Pitti Filati for yarn, and Linea Pelle for leather. These shows provide a wealth of contacts and agents for sourcing fabrics, trims, and specialist details. Although most manufacturers are initially unwilling to deal with students—due to the small quantities being ordered—it is possible to buy from stock sampling if the minimum order is agreeable. Agents may also hold some sample stock that needs to be cleared at the end of the buying season. The Première Vision directory contains valuable information on manufacturers, contact details, fabric types, and so on. You should also consider visiting mills and any local suppliers, as these sources often provide high-quality fabrics at lower costs.

Market level

All fashion has a market level, regardless of the type or occasion. If you feel you have no competitors or that no one else is making a similar product (in terms of cost or type), then you need to research further. Although aesthetics and creativity are defined by each designer or manufacturer, a visit to a high-quality department store, in the concessions or designer area, will show you how market-level definitions are made and stocked at the business end of fashion.

7   Camille Hardwick –
    The Festival Dress '14.

FESTIVAL '14

THIS FESTIVAL SEASON, THE URBAN OUTFITTERS GIRL
CHARTS HER PATH ACROSS THE GLOBE FOLLOWING THE
MUSIC. FASHION COMES FIRST SO LOOKING EFFORT-
LESSLY GORGEOUS IS THE CHIEF OBJECTIVE.

ARTS THREAD **UO** URBAN OUTFITTERS

7

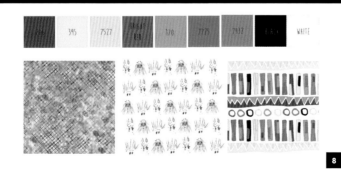

8

8   Camille Hardwick –
    pantone colors and
    print design.

The brief

9 Camille Hardwick –
print and silhouette.

9

10 Camille Hardwick – mood and color.

10

11 Anna Yates-Housley – portfolio.
    "Claustrophobia," A/W 2014.

151

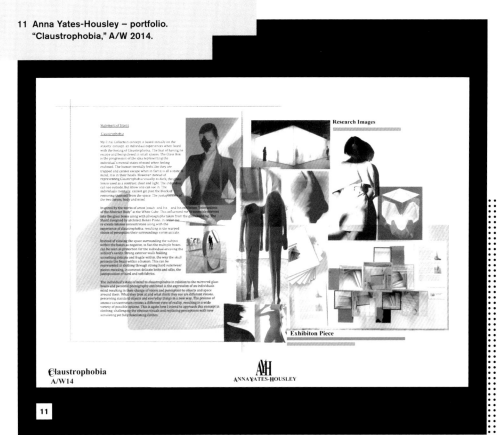

YOUR PORTFOLIO

Your portfolio will ultimately secure your first job or a place in a postgraduate course. Within your portfolio, you should show the process and outcome of your final collection—through edited research and development, images, and photographs of the final outfits. If you have shown your collection in a static or catwalk show, include good-quality images from the event to showcase your work as professionally as possible.

A comprehensive portfolio will contain at least six projects, covering a range of activities and different types of design work. Be sure to include examples of color development, IT applications, technical drawings, range plans, any industry-linked work, use of textiles, and so on. Most professional portfolios feature a list of contents and page breaks to section off each project. If you wish to produce a digital portfolio, remember that anyone looking at this will not be able to touch fabrics or trims as part of the viewing (which is also true of plastic sleeves). Keep your portfolio clean, ensure that it is manageable and easily portable, and be prepared to update it or reconfigure it, depending on the type of interview.

Your portfolio

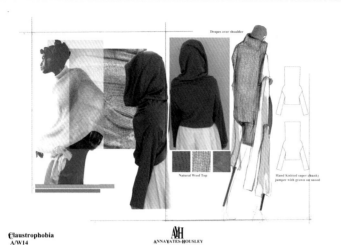

Drapes over shoulder

Natural Wool Top

Hand Knitted super chunky jumper with grown on snood

Claustrophobia
A/W14

AYH
ANNA YATES-HOUSLEY

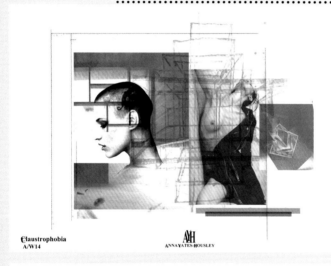

Claustrophobia
A/W14

AYH
ANNA YATES-HOUSLEY

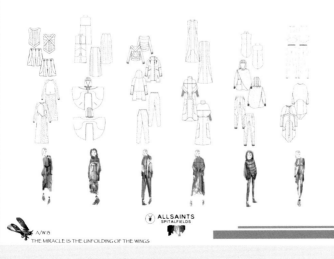

A/W13
THE MIRACLE IS THE UNFOLDING OF THE WINGS

ALLSAINTS
SPITALFIELDS

The student collection

12 Anna Yates-Housley. The inspiration behind the "Claustrophobia" collection was based on the anxiety disorder of the same name. The concept challenges classic views of clothing and replaces these perceptions with new, stimulating yet fully functioning clothes. The collection works in oversized, elongated and multi-functional layers building up around the body with a heavy focus on outerwear.

YOUR PORTFOLIO SHOULD INCLUDE:

Illustrations

Technical drawings (flats)

Sample board of fabric, trims, and finishes

Initial research boards

Photographs of final garments, either from a photo shoot or catwalk show

Final lookbook of collection

Press cuttings, CVs, and business cards

Look at how magazines lay out images and text. Study books on related design subjects, such as graphic or textile design, architecture, furniture, and product design. Upmarket catalogs or leaflets from cosmetic, electronic, and car manufacturers are often beautifully produced with huge financial budgets. Study these and deconstruct how and why they look so effective and beautiful. Once you can identify this process and methodology to powerful two-dimensional imagery, you can transfer this thinking to your own work with powerful, confident results.

Drawing

Drawing is a fundamental process in visual communication, from initial quick reference sketches to fully rendered illustrations. Most fashion courses look for evidence of drawing in interview portfolios.

However, drawing has become a much wider descriptor in the fashion industry, which requires technical drawing, range planning, and specification documents. The development of various software packages has enabled fashion students to replicate a number of industry standard processes and techniques when presenting fashion ideas and collections.

Research materials

It is commonplace to include evidence of source materials and all research activities, which will constitute the main part of your portfolio. This provides evidence of your skills related to research, development, and presentation of materials. A sound portfolio should contain a minimum of five to six projects to encompass variety, product differences, color, print, silhouette, occasion, and so on. It is important to show a design identity, as well as creative diversity. Be rigorous and present an edited, considered representation of the whole process. Too little work will look scant and poorly informed. Too much will look confused and busy.

13 Krista Hendriksen. Mood board exploring the fascinating shapes produced by jelly moulds.

RESEARCH AND DEVELOPMENT

Research will form the basis for your collection, and you will need to gather an exhaustive range of source materials. These will include specific investigations into fabrics, color, silhouette shapes, and details, as well as live events and imagery in the form of drawings and photographs—in fact, a broad coverage of everything that will inform and influence your thinking and decision making. As you go on to develop your collection, which involves editing, refining, and amending your initial proposals, it is important that you have enough research to allow for this. The visual presentation and collation of this body of work should illustrate the breadth and detail of your thinking in an exciting and dynamic way. This is vital, as you will revisit this stage of the project as you progress toward the later stages. Visual materials should speak for themselves and illustrate your thinking and development.

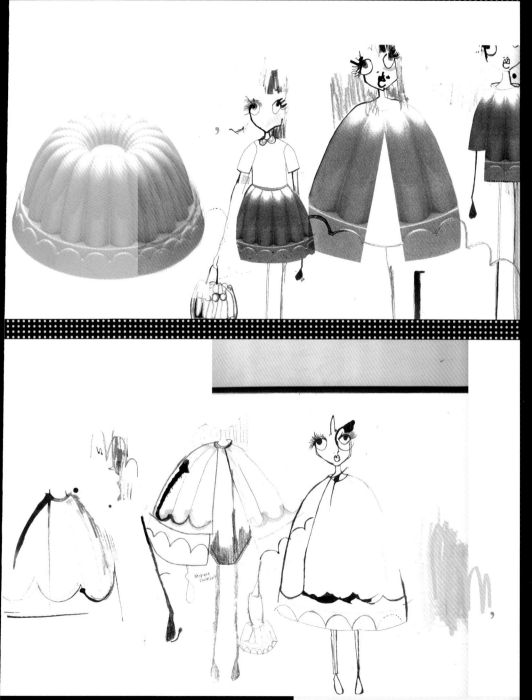

14 Krista Hendriksen – the development process.

15, 16 Héléna Denize, *École de la Chambre Syndicale de la Couture Parisienne.*

Sourcing

Try to avoid downloading simplistic images from websites or using too many tear sheets from popular magazines, as this usually equates to a perception that you could have done more work elsewhere. There is no substitute for discovery and innovation through primary research.

Consider compiling your research into various categories—inspiration, color, fabrics, shapes, and accessories. You may find it useful to write a short story or narrative that explains your process or defines the overall approach.

Try creating characters or situations from history, fantasy, or everyday life to provide a basis for your research. You may be inspired by a book or a film. If so, investigate more about the author, theory, or context by looking at other related examples. Keep a small notebook with you for notes and sketches. Take the time to go to vintage shops and markets, or even auction websites, such as eBay or Etsy, as these are a valuable source of original garments to dissect and rework. Museums or galleries also offer the best initial contact with inspirational materials.

Write letters or emails for appointments to discuss your project with the experts or connections to the materials you need. If you are interested in using color to make your collection memorable, research established colorists in fashion and textiles and consider what you could learn from their successes.

Great designers are fastidious on research and detail, with collections referenced in full. The more preparation and investigation put into this stage, the better prepared you will be when you have to make subsequent decisions or undertake more specific research and sourcing.

Designing from your research

This stage of the process, known as design development, bridges your research into the final outcome. As such, this stage will involve working with the key aspects of your research—images, drawings, fabrics, and so on—and interpreting them in your designs. Drawing together each detail, it is possible through thought and reflection to assemble a series of drawings, photographs, and collages that will contain your preferences and ideas allocated to each piece and outfit.

It is important to remain flexible and open to change, as ideas may not work as initially thought, or availability of fabrics may change. Use drawings and photographs as an easy visual resource to explore ideas and permutations.

Realization

At this stage, you will be moving into the realization of your ideas—through pattern making and creating toiles, draping, and constructing the first samples. You may also be printing and knitting samples that will be used as a part of the final presentation of your collection. You now should be sourcing and organizing your trims, ordering fabrics, and perhaps working with additional producers—knitters, printers, accessory designers, and jewelers.

Project managing

Consider drawing up a production chart or critical path for each piece of your collection. This will help you manage your time and make decisions when problems occur. It is always a good idea to have an initial line-up or range plan so you can remind yourself of tasks completed and those areas that are more time hungry. You need to see the whole project coming together against time constraints, critical deadlines, and input from your teachers. You should be prepared for disasters and aspects that don't go to plan, such as fabrics that are out of stock or toiles that don't work. Perhaps some work takes longer than planned, or there may be hidden costs and promises that fail to materialize. These are difficulties that designers and producers encounter all the time; although difficult, these challenges can be overcome while preserving your vision and planning. Try to remain flexible and positive throughout.

Documenting and preserving research

Be prepared and photograph your toiles, fittings, and stand work. Photographs will provide you with a clear record of your development and any refinements needed as part of this process. You can also plan for a review or critique with tutors or other students by using your photographs as part of your range plan or collection line-up.

Remember to keep records of fabrics, trims, and anything related to each garment. The photographs and drawings will illustrate only part of the story, and it is difficult to envisage some toiles in the finished (or proposed) fabric.

Your drawings, swatches, samples, and prototypes should convey a clear message, but they may be experimental and can always be rethought or discussed. Your two-dimensional work and three-dimensional development should be allowed to evolve; don't resist drawing on a toile or photograph to keep your imagination stimulated and your judgment sharp.

Reviewing

Ensure that you are prepared and ready to present your work at review points. This is an opportunity to discuss your work and should be challenging yet constructive. While it is important and helpful to be able to present your research visually and verbally, the story being told should ideally work without the need for verbal explanation. Any discussion sections or reviews will, of course, involve conversation, advice, and an exchange of viewpoints, but if you find yourself explaining your research at length, then perhaps you do not have enough visual research, or it may be muddled. The final portfolio and collection presentation will not be accompanied by a verbal narrative, and it will succeed or fail on its ability to communicate to the audience.

Remember, you are telling a story through images and finished outcomes. Images, drawings, fabrics, and activities should be carefully placed and related to specifics, so don't, for example, show an image and then the final collection. Taking time to prepare at this stage is invaluable and will help you get the most from presenting and discussing your work.

Make yourself aware of what is expected, who will be part of this review, and what you hope to gain from it. If you have questions relating

17 Jean Philippe Chemin.

17

to your work, write them down, and if the points are not covered as part of the review, ask for a few moments at the end. Successful reviews are based on a dialogue, so although you may feel nervous (or worried if you know you are behind schedule), know that, for your progression, your teachers want to work with you to arrive at the best possible outcome.

Throughout the review process, editing will be expected: for example, an idea may be better developed within another garment or outfit, or you may have to select from looks that are becoming repetitive. At this point, the rejected elements will have to be replaced, based on the development of the rest of the collection. This process is evolutionary, and it reflects professional practice. It is almost impossible to plan and systemize the entire process without revising and reworking ideas.

Research and development

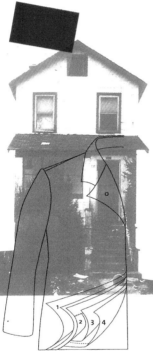

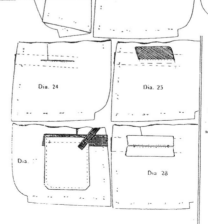

► LES TISSUS DE RENFORT

0. LES PARMENTURES sont les pièces de tissu qui
suivent la ligne de coupe et permettent de finir
les montants des boutons, les ourlets, l'encolure,
les entournures et les poignets d'un vêtement
en retournant le bord cousu vers l'intérieur.
Les parmentures peuvent également être coupées
dans des tissus décoratifs.

1. LES ENTOILAGES sont des tissus spécialisés,
cousus ou thermocollés sur les revers ou sur
du tissu pour donner à ceux-ci plus de tenue
aux endroits critiques, tels que les montants
des boutons, les cols et les manchettes.

2. LES DOUBLURES INTÉGRÉES sont utilisées pour
renforcer un tissu léger, ou pour réduire sa
transparence. On les coupe à partir des mêmes
pièces de patron que les pièces visibles, et on
les coud à ces dernières avant de commencer
l'assemblage. Ainsi, au moment de construire
le vêtement, on traite comme une seule entité
la doublure intégrée et le tissu apparent.

3. LES DOUBLURES. On les utilise pour donner
un aspect fini à l'intérieur d'un vêtement façon

trop large. Pour le cuir, utilisez de plus longues aiguille
Employez des aiguilles pour le cuir ou des aiguilles M
imperméables comme le Goretex et les nylons pour
de secours dans une petite boîte, enveloppées dans
paire de pinces peuvent s'avérer utiles si l'on se sert
la règle d'or concernant le choix du fil, est d'en

PLATE 47
Splitting 7, 1975
Two gelatin silver prints, cut and collaged
21 x 31 in. (53.3 x 78.7 cm)
Collection of Frederieke Sanders Taylor

18   Jean Philippe Chemin.

18

PRESENTATION

The final collection, a lookbook and all source, research, and development materials, will comprise your final submission or presentation. The final collection in three dimensions will be specified to your course requirements, but it will usually be displayed on a rail and arranged in complete outfits or looks. You may also have to include patterns, toiles, specification sheets, or costings and technical files to support the collection and evidence the process from start to finish. Different fashion-based courses have specific requirements that reflect the curriculum content or specialization.

Designer collections can be anything upward of fifteen looks or outfits. An undergraduate student will typically produce a prototype collection of six outfits as a part of a college show. Postgraduate fashion students may produce twelve to fifteen outfits. These typical figures reflect the scheduled student timetables and the students' skills and level of experience. In addition, whereas most designers' shows run for a maximum of twenty to twenty-five minutes, undergraduate fashion shows will run for no more than forty-five to fifty minutes, so six outfits is generally acknowledged as an adequate number of outfits for each student to convey the theme and content of the collection (and it also allows enough time for the show to feature the selected students).

Graduate fashion shows

Most student shows will have a running order of twenty to thirty students (known as *exits* in designer shows), although many fashion-based courses are much larger.

A selection process takes place in nearly all fashion colleges for a press or event-based show (such as Graduate Fashion Week in London), and each college will have its own criteria for selecting the final show order. Often a panel of judges is convened to view the range of collections that will make for the best show possible. Judges will be looking for cohesive, well-cut, and well-finished clothes that will contain enough visual narrative to tell a story or communicate to the audience.

KRISTA HENDRIKSEN

19 **Krista Hendriksen – line-up.**

The student collection

20 Graduate Fashion Week in London, 2014.

There is no formula for certainty in this selection. If a number of students have, for example, produced a range of black jersey womenswear separates, it is unlikely that, given a choice, all collections will make the final running order. No college wants to show a lack of creative diversity and run the risk of an unhappy audience or negative press coverage. Likewise, it is unlikely that a complete show will be entirely made up of hugely dramatic, theatrical clothes, as this is unrepresentative of fashion as a whole. Beautifully crafted, effortless clothes are irresistible and make for a great show—even if they are not entirely for everyday wear.

Study web-based media to read show reviews, and where possible, look at college websites and DVDs to see examples of choice and show presentation. Remember, however, that although a show can be a great profile builder or press focus, your portfolio is arguably as important for your future.

Presentation

21 Lauren Lake. Pink shearling jacket inspired by
the expeditions of Scott of the Antarctic.

The lookbook

The lookbook or visual line-up will show each of the outfits on models or arranged to convey the intended fashion story.
A lookbook is a photographic range plan produced by designers, manufacturers, and retailers each season or for each fashion story. Sometimes the fashion looks are photographed from a catwalk show or as individual pieces—such as accessories and footwear. The books are designed to assist buyers in making their choices and to merchandise across their buying budget. Retailers use lookbooks to recreate in-store merchandise stories and as visual aids for windows or displays. Your version is intended to convey your complete fashion look or story. Styled photographs work well, but however you illustrate your work, it should be clear and informative and link together. The images should convey the complete design process leading up to the final outcome.

22 Sadie Clayton – lookbook. This shimmering dress was one of six looks created by Sadie for the Graduate Fashion Week.

22

Presentation

23

24

23, 24 Phoebe Kowalska layers
neoprene and nylon to create
protective clothing.

25 Amy Heath – Graduate Fashion Week.

25

Styling

You should consider the styling and total look possible within any fashion range. While it is easy to design footwear, accessories, and jewelry on paper, it is fairly straightforward to customize inexpensive or thrift shop finds. These additional pieces can be key to the overall design statement—at times they can propel a range of garments into an innovative fashion statement through humor, drama, color, or whimsy. This consideration also confirms your attention to detail and ability to direct a complete fashion statement.

When planning and constructing a styling shoot, you should research and plan for the overall look you are trying to achieve. A good starting point is to gather a selection of high-quality magazines aimed at a variety of readers. Acne *i-D, Self Service, Jocks & Nerds, Another Magazine, A Magazine,* and American *Vogue* are just a few examples of magazines that feature the industry's best photographers, makeup artists, and stylists. Each photographic image has been painstakingly constructed, styled, lit, and photographed. The best styling images convey a clear, powerful message. In fashion, this usually emphasizes an aspect of the clothes being photographed (such as silhouette, proportion, scale, volume, color, and so on), or a dynamic contrast where hugely expensive garments are featured in unusual settings. Having begun to understand how styled images are configured, you are better prepared to create your own.

CONCLUSION

This book has taken you on a journey through the various processes and expectations when trying to develop a collection.

Starting with the key processes involved in researching, designing, and producing a collection, this book will also help you understand how the different roles within a team come together to develop a collection, be it for a main collection or a specialist collection, such as knitwear, childrenswear, or accessories. Mainly focusing on womenswear and menswear, designers' influences are identified into social categories, including historical, cultural, functional, political, artistic, and futuristic.

The main text is supported by contemporary interviews with a diverse cross section of global designers working in the fashion industry, which we hope will inspire you to realize your aspirations as the next generation of designers.

26 Stunning menswear from the E. Tautz Fall/Winter 2014 collection, featuring hand embroidery by undergraduate degree students from the Royal School of Needlework, UK.

Index

A

accessories, 9, 126–127
achieving aspiration, 148
Acne *i-D*, 167
active sportswear, 124
actors as muses, 21
A Magazine, 167
Amendola, Louis, 76–77
American Gigolo, 21
Another Magazine, 167
Antwerp Academy of Fine Arts, 56
Antwerp Six, 56, 57
Apparelsourcing, 24
archiving collections, 28–29
Armani, Giorgio, 21, 36
    haute couture, 90, 93
artifacts, 18
artistic influences, 72–73
Ashley, Laura, 12
A Single Man, 21
ASOS (As Seen on Screen), 106
ateliers, 90
availability of stock, 12

B

bags, 126–127
Baldwin, Alexandra, 146
Balenciaga, Cristóbal, 38, 53, 59
Bates, Joe, 110–111
Beene, Geoffrey, 70
Beirendonck, Walter Van, 56
Berry, Holly, 28
Beyoncé, 101
Bikkembergs, Dirk, 56
blankets, 104
blocks, 32
Bodymap, 124
brands
    designers, 123. *See also*
        designers
    knitwear, 123
Breakfast at Tiffany's, 21
briefs, student collections, 144–146
Brooks Brothers, 21, 102
Broome, Will, 86–87
Bryan, Sid, 49, 110–111
Burberry, 21, 64
Burstein, Joan, 34
buyers, 34
    market research for, 12

C

Campbell, Edie, 20
capsule collections, 38
Cardin, Pierre, 70, 99

Cary-Williams, Robert, 65
catwalks
    showpieces, 15, 17
    shows, 39–41
celebrity collaborations, 101
Chalayan, Hussein, 62, 63, 102, 124
Chambre Syndicale de la Haute
        Couture, 70, 90
Chanel, 11, 21, 59
    haute couture markets, 90
    ready-to-wear collections, 94
Chanel, Coco, 94
character merchandise, 120
Chemin, Jean Phillippe, 159–161
childrenswear, 120–121
Clayton, Sadie, 165
Cocteau, Jean, 72
Cohen, Charli, 134–135
collaborations
    celebrity, 101
    designers, 100
collections
    archiving, 28–29
    buyers, 34
    capsule, 38
    catwalk shows, 39–41
    creativity *versus* wearability, 17
    definition of, 9
    designers, 30–32
    development, 22–24
    editing, 29
    fabric sourcing, 24–25
    forecasting trends, 26–27
    haute couture, 91
    high-street, 102–106, 121
    identifying customers, 15–17
    influences of, 55–88. *See also*
        influences
    inspiration, 18–21
    lookbooks, 38
    market research, 11, 12
    merchandisers, 34
    pattern cutters, 32–33
    PR (public relation) agents,
        34–35
    product developers, 34
    ready-to-wear, 94–95
    research, 11
    resources, 35–36
    sample cutters, 33
    sample machinists, 33
    showing, 36–38
    specialist, 119–142. *See also*
        specialist collections
    starting, 11

student, 143–169. *See also*
        student collections
    studio managers, 33
    stylists, 34–35
    teams, 30–35
color boards, 19
companies, trend, 26–27
competition, student collections, 147
comp shop, 12
conceptual fashion, 62–64
corporate wear, 125
costs of student collections, 148
Council for Designers in America
        (CFDA), 96
Courrèges, André, 70
creativity
    context of, 144
    versus wearability, 17
cultural references, 18, 55, 60–61
customers
    identifying, 15–17
    profiles, 15
    student collections, 146

D

Dali, Salvador, 36, 72
darts, placement of, 32
databases, 28
Davies, George, 107
Deacon, Giles, 100, 108–109
de Castelbajac, Jean-Charles, 68
de la Falaise, Loulou, 21
Delevingne, Cara, 21, 123
delivery of stock, 12
Demeulemeester, Ann, 56
Deneuve, Catherine, 21
Denize, Héléna, 156
design direction, 9
designers, 30–32
    adopting new, 12
    blocks, 32
    childrenswear, 120
    collaborations, 100
    collections. *See* collections
    footwear, 127
    identifying customers, 15–17
    influences, 55–88. *See also*
        influences
    inspiration, 18–21
    interviews. *See* interviews
    labels, 96–98
designing for markets, 89–118. *See*
        also markets
development
    archiving, 28–29

buyers, 34
capsule, 38
catwalk shows, 39–41
creativity *versus* wearability, 17
definition of, 9
designers, 30–32
editing, 29
fabric sourcing, 24–25
forecasting trends, 26–27
haute couture, 91
high-street, 102–106, 121
identifying customers, 15–17
influences of, 55–88. *See also*
        influences
inspiration, 18–21
lookbooks, 38
market research, 11, 12
merchandisers, 34
pattern cutters, 32–33
PR (public relation) agents, 4–35
product developers, 34
ready-to-wear, 94–95
research, 11
resources, 35–36
sample cutters, 33
sample machinists, 33
showing, 36–38
specialist, 119–142. *See also*
        specialist collections
starting, 11
student, 143–169. *See also*
        student collections
studio managers, 33
stylists, 34–35
teams, 30–35
de Vos, Christopher, 100
Dior, 30
    haute couture markets, 90
    ready-to-wear collections, 94
Dior, Christian, 94
documenting research, 158
Dover, Poppy, 19
drawing, student collections, 153
Dr Noki, 78–79
drops, 102
Dundas, Peter, 58

E
Edelkoort, Li, 44
editing collections, 29
Elbaz, Alber, 59
Elle, 56
environmental influences, 55
Everlast, 123
exclusivity, 12

F
fabric
    fairs, 24
    market research, 12
    student collections, 148
    swatches, 18
FAD Competition, 146
Fashion East, 96
Fashion Fringe, 96
fibers, 123
Field Grey, 125
film, 21
fit models, 22
fittings, 32
flous, 90
footwear, 126–127
Ford, Tom, 21
forecasting trends, 26–27
found pieces, 18
Fox, Shelley, 37, 44–45
Franklin, Cary, 68
Fraser, Graham, 66
freelance designers, 22. *See also*
        designers
Fulton, Holly, 46–47
functional garments, 65–66
furniture, 127
futuristic influences, 70–71

G
Galliano, John, 15, 17, 21, 34
    haute couture, 91
garments, 9. *See also* collections
    functional, 65–66
    teams. *See* teams (collections)
Gere, Richard, 21
Ghesquière, Nicolas, 38, 58
Gibb, Bill, 123
Givenchy, Hubert de, 21
    haute couture markets, 90
graduate fashion shows, 162–164
Graves, Michael, 100
The Great Gatsby, 21
Green, Sir Philip, 101
Greenyer, Katie, 80–81
grids, 28
Gucci, 99

H
Halston, 125
Hamnett, Katharine, 102
hardware, 127
Hardwick, Camille, 149, 150
Harlech, Lady Amanda, 21

haute couture
    ateliers, 90
    collections, 11, 91
    future of, 92–93
    markets, 90–93
    origins of, 90
Heather, Amy, 167
Hemingway, Wayne, 29
Hendriksen, Krista, 154, 155
Hepburn, Audrey, 12
Hidalgo, Alex, 53
high-street collections,
        102–106, 121
Hiroshima Chic, 56
historical references, 18, 55, 56,
        58–59
H&M, 102
house models, 22
Hulme, Sophie, 82–83, 146

I
identifying customers, 15–17
influences, 55–88
    artistic, 72–73
    conceptual fashion, 62–64
    cultural references, 60–61
    functional garments, 65–66
    futuristic, 70–71
    historical references, 56,
        58–59
    political references, 68–69
    workwear, 67
inspiration for collections, 18–21
interviews
    Amendola, Louis, 76–77
    Broome, Will, 86–87
    Cohen, Charli, 134–135
    Deacon, Giles, 108–109
    Dr Noki, 78–79
    Fox, Shelley, 44–45
    Fulton, Holly, 46–47
    Greenyer, Katie, 80–81
    Hulme, Sophie, 82–83
    Karayiannis, Eva, 128–132
    Kirkwood, Nicholas, 138–139
    Leutton, Jenny, 132–133
    Llanos, Felipe Rojas, 52–53
    Lynn, Todd, 48–49
    MacKenzie, Kenneth, 84–85
    McNair, Colin, 112–113
    Mooney, John, 116–117
    Mulligan, Tracy, 136–137
    Nicoll, Richard, 50–51
    Raymond, Martin, 42–43
    Richardson, Gordon, 114–115

Ruuger, Oliver, 140–141
SIBLING, 110–111
Stuart, Fiona, 74–75

J
Jackson, Betty, 102
Jacobs, Marc, 58, 72
James, Marcus, 49
Jocks & Nerds, 167

K
Kamali, Norma, 124
Karayiannis, Eva, 128–132
Kawakubo, Rei, 56, 62
Kennedy, Lulu, 50
Kirkwood, Nicholas, 138–139
Kishimoto, Eley, 127
Klein, Calvin, 12, 65
Klein, Yves, 146
Knight, Nick, 36
knitwear, 122–123
Kowalska, Phoebe, 166
Kusama, Yoyoi, 72

L
labels, 11, 96–98. *See also*
    collections
Lagerfeld, Karl, 21, 59. *See also*
    Chanel
    haute couture, 90
Lake, Lauren, 164
Land of Lost Content museum, 29
Lang, Helmut, 62
Lanvin, 59
lasts, 127
Laugesen, Jens, 29
Lauren, Ralph, 12, 54
Leutton, Jenny, 132–133
levels, markets, 89. *See also* markets
Lewis, John, 100
Linea Pelle (fabric fair), 25
Llanos, Felipe Rojas, 52–53
lookbooks, 38
    student collections, 165–167
Louboutin, Christian, 49
Louis Vuitton, 39, 40, 41, 59
Luhrmann, Baz, 21
luxury brands, 99
Lynn, Todd, 22, 48–49

M
MacDonald, Julien, 102
MacKenzie, Kenneth, 84–85
Madonna, 101
magazines, 167
manufacturers, 22, 103
Margiela, Martin, 56
    haute couture, 90
markets
    celebrity collaborations, 101
    childrenswear, 121
    designer collaborations, 100
    designer labels, 96–98
    designing for, 89–118
    haute couture, 90–93

high-street collections, 102–106
luxury brands, 99
online shopping, 106–107
ready-to-wear collections, 94–95
researching collections, 11, 12
student collections, 148
Marks and Spencer, 102, 121
Martin, Catherine, 21
Massenet, Natalie, 106
McCardell, Claire, 67
McCartney, Stella, 68, 106, 124
McCreery, Cozette, 110–111
McNair, Colin, 112–113
McQueen, Alexander, 17, 48, 56
merchandisers, 34
Messe Frankfurt (fabric fair), 24
Meyer-Wiel, Georg, 18
milliners, 17
mills, fabric, 24. *See also* fabric
Minogue, Kylie, 101
Missoni, Ottavio, 122
Missoni, Rosita, 122
Miyake, Issey, 62, 123
Mizrahi, Isaac, 100
models
    house, 22
    as muses, 21
Montana, Claude, 48
mood boards, 18, 19
Mooney, John, 116–117
Moss, Kate, 101
Mouret, Roland, 48, 106
Mulberry, 21, 100
Mulligan, Tracy, 136–137
muses, 20, 21. *See also* inspiration
    for collections

N
Net-a-Porter, 106
Next Directory, 107
Nicoll, Richard, 50–51
Nott, Richard, 66

O
Oldham, Todd, 100
Olympic activewear, 124
online shopping, 106–107
Orta, Lucy, 36

P
Paris, France, 38
    Chambre Syndicale de la Haute
        Couture, 70, 90
    fabric fairs, 24
Parsons School, 67
pattern cutters, 32–33
Philo, Phoebe, 127
photographic archiving, 28
Pilotto, Peter, 100
Pitti Bimbo, 121
Pitti Filati, 24
planning collections, 11
    archiving, 28–29
    catwalk shows, 39–41

creativity *versus* wearability, 17
    development, 22–24
    editing, 29
    fabric sourcing, 24–25
    forecasting trends, 26–27
    identifying customers, 15–17
    lookbooks, 38
    market research, 12
    teams, 30–35
political influences, 55
political references, 68–69
Popp, Lucinda, 24
portfolios, student collections,
    151–153
Prada, 21
PR (public relation) agents, 34–35
pre-collections, 11
premières, 90
Première Vision, 24, 25, 44, 148
presentations, student collections,
    162–164
preserving research, 158
prêt-à-porter. *See* ready-to-wear
    collections
prices, market research, 12
products, 9. *See also* collections
    developers, 34
profiles, customers, 15
project managing, 158
Pucci, Emilio, 58, 125
Pugh, Gareth, 36
Pullman, Jeffrey, 51
Puma, 124

Q
quality of merchandise, 12

R
Rabanne, Paco, 70
rails, 28
range building, 105
Raymond, Martin, 42–43
ready-to-wear collections, 11,
    94–95
Rendez-Vous, 38
research
    collections, 11
    designing from, 157
    documenting, 158
    preserving, 158
    realization, 158
    reviewing, 158
    sourcing, 157
    student collections, 153,
        154–161
resources
    collections, 35–36
    magazines, 167
retail
    collections, 22. *See also*
        collections
    designer collaborations, 100
    online shopping, 106–107
Rhode, Nancy, 45

Developing a Fashion Collection

Richardson, Gordon, 114–115
rigging, 105
Rocha, John, 125
Ruuger, Oliver, 140–141
Rykiel, Sonia, 122

S
Saab, Ellie, 93
safety considerations, 121
Saint Laurent, Yves, 19, 21, 30, 31,
    48, 60, 67
    influences, 72
    luxury brands, 99
    ready-to-wear collections, 94
sample cutters, 33
sample machinists, 33
Sander, Jill, 62, 100
Sanderson, Chris, 42
Savile Row tailors, 33
schedules, collections, 36
Schiaparelli, Elsa, 36
Scott, Jeremy, 68
seam lines, placement of, 32
Self Service, 167
Shanghai, China, 24
Shima Seiki, 122
shoes, 126–127
showing collections, 36–38
SIBLING, 110–111
skills, student collections, 146
Slimane, Hedi, 20
Smedley, John, 44
sourcing, 157
special collections, 11
specialist collections, 119–142
    accessories, 126–127
    active sportswear, 124
    bags, 126–127
    childrenswear, 120–121
    corporate wear, 125
    footwear, 126–127
    knitwear, 122–123
Stuart, Fiona, 74–75
student collections, 143–169
    achieving aspirations, 148
    briefs, 144–146

competition, 147
costs, 148
customers, 146
designing from research, 157
drawing, 153
fabric, 148
graduate fashion shows,
    162–164
lookbooks, 165–167
markets, 148
portfolios, 151–153
presentations, 162–164
project managing, 158
realization, 158
research, 153, 154–161
reviewing, 158
skills, 146
sourcing, 157
styling, 167
studio managers, 33
styling, student collections, 167
stylists, 34–35
suppliers for high-street collections,
    103
swatches (fabric), 18

T
tailleurs, 90
tailors, Savile Row, 33
Target, 100
Tautz, E., 168
teams (collections), 30–35
    buyers, 34
    designers, 30–32
    merchandisers, 34
    pattern cutters, 32–33
    PR (public relation) agents,
        34–35
    product developers, 34
    sample cutters, 33
    sample machinists, 33
    studio managers, 33
    stylists, 34–35
tear sheets, 18
technical packages, 105
Temperley, Alice, 100

textiles, 24. See also fabric
Texworld, 24
themes, 9
Thorp, Aitor, 36
Throup, Aitor, 70
Tissu Lille (fabric fair), 25
toiles, 32, 33
Topshop, 96, 102
Treacy, Phillip, 17
trends, 9, 26–27
Trenois, 38
trims, 148. See also fabric
Tschirky, Stefanie, 144
Turkish Fabric Fair, 25

U
Uniqlo, 100

V
Valentino, haute couture, 90, 93
Van Noten, Dries, 56
Van Saene, Dirk, 56
Varvatos, John, 112
vendeuse (saleswoman), 91
Versace, Gianni, 56
Vogue, 167
Vogue Fashion Fund, 96

W
Wang, Alexander, 106
wearability, creativity versus, 17
Westwood, Vivienne, 56, 125
Wetherell, Sophie, 143
WGSN (forecasting agency), 26
Williamson, Matthew, 102
wool, 123
workwear, 67

Y
Yamamoto, Yohji, 62
Yarn Expo, 24
yarns, 123, 148. See also fabric
Yates-Housley, Anna, 151, 152
Yee, Marina, 56
YSL brand, 99. See also Saint
    Laurent, Yves

Shops and markets

:::

London shops

Absolute Vintage
15 Hanbury Street
London E1 6QR
www.absolutevintage.co.uk

Anthropologie
158 Regent Street
London W1B 5SW
www.anthropologie.com

A.P.C.
40 Dover Street Market
London W1S 4LT
www.apc.fr

Bang Bang
(Womenswear)
21 Goodge Street
London W1T 2PJ
www.bangbangclothingexchange.co.uk

Beyond Retro
110–112 Cheshire Street
London E2 6EJ
www.beyondretro.com

Beyond the Valley
2 Newburgh Street
London W1F 7RD

Blackout II
(Vintage clothing and accessories)
51 Endell Street
London WC2H 9AJ
www.blackout2.com

Browns
24–27 South Molton Street
London W1K 5RD
www.brownsfashion.com

Browns Focus
24 South Molton Street
London W1K 5RN
http://www.brownsfashion.com/info/stores/
browns-focus

Concrete
35a Marshall Street
London W1F

Dover Street Market
17–18 Dover Street
London W1S 4LT
www.doverstreetmarket.com

Feathers
40 Hans Crescent
London SW1X OLZ

Hostem
41–43 Redchurch Street
London E2 7DL
www.hostem.co.uk

Hoxton Boutique
2 Hoxton Street
London N1
www.hoxtonboutique.com

Issey Miyake
52 Conduit Street
London W1S 2YX
www.isseymiyake.com

Koh Samui
65 Monmouth Street
London WC2H 9DG
www.kohsamui.co.uk

Kokon to Zai
57 Greek Street
London W1D 3DX
www.kokontozai.co.uk

Liberty
Regent Street
W1B 5AH
www.liberty.co.uk

The Library
(Menswear)
268 Brompton Road
London SW3 2AS
www.thelibrary1994.com

LN-CC
(Appointment only)
18 Shacklewell Lane
Dalston
London E8 2EZ
www.ln-cc.com

Maison Martin Margiela
22 Bruton Street
London W1J 6NE
www.maisonmartinmargiela.com

Marni
16 Sloane Street
London SW1X 9NE
www.marni.com

Matches
60–64 Ledbury Road
London W11 2AJ
www.matchesfashion.com

Modern Age Vintage
65 Chalk Farm Road
NW1 8AN
www.modern-age.co.uk

The Observatory
20 Greenwich Church Street
London SE10

Present
(Menswear)
140 Shoreditch High Street
London E1 6JE
www.present-london.com

Rellik
Golbourne Road
London W10 5NW
www.relliklondon.co.uk

Retro Man & Retro woman
32–34 Pembridge Rd
W11 3HN
www.mgeshops.com

Rick Owens
64 South Audley Street
London W1K 2QT
www.rickowens.eu

Selfridges
400 Oxford Street
London W1A 1AB
www.selfridges.com

The Shop at Bluebird
350 Kings Road
London SW3 5UU
www.theshopatbluebird.co.uk

Sonia Rykiel
27–29 Brook Street
London W1K 4HD
www.soniarykiel.com

Start
59 Rivington Street
London EC2
www.start-london.com

Urban Outfitters
200–201 Oxford Street
London W1D 1NU
www.urbanoutfitters.co.uk

Vivienne Westwood
6 Davies Street
London W1K 3DN
www.viviennewestwood.com

Yohji Yamamoto
14–15 Conduit Street
London W1S 2XJ
www.yohjiyamamoto.co.jp

Shops and markets

New York shops

Acustom Apparel
(Independent)
330 West Broadway
New York, NY 10013
www.acustom.com

Balenciaga
148 Mercer Street
New York, NY 10012
www.balenciaga.com

Boutique Ludivine
172 West 4th Street
New York, NY 10009
www.boutiqueludivine.com

Darling
(Independent)
1 Horatio Street
New York, NY 10014
www.darlingnyc.com

J. Mendel
787 Maddison Avenue
New York, NY 10065
www.jmendel.com

Kiwi Design Co.
(Independent)
119 7th Avenue
Brooklyn, NY 11215
www.kiwidesignco.com

Otte-Nolita
281 Mott Street
New York, NY 10012
www.otteny.com

Pas de Deux
(Independent)
328 East 11th Street
New York, NY 10003
www.pasdedeuxny.com

Paris shops

Catherine B
(Independent)
1 et 3, rue Guisande
75006
Paris
www.catherine-b.com

Citadium
50 rue Caumartin
75009
Paris
www.citadium.com

L'Eclaireur
40 rue de Sévigné
75003
Paris
www.leclaireur.com

Isabel Marant
16 rue de Charome
75011
Paris
www.isabelmarant.com

Philippe Janssers
(Independent)
3 Rue d'Anjou
75008
Paris

Spree
16 rue La Vieuville
75018
Montmartre
Paris
www.spree.fr

London markets

Brick Lane Market
Brick Lane
Cheshire Street
and Sclater Street
London E1

Brixton Market
(Thursday to Sunday
from 9:30am–5.30pm)
Electric Avenue
Pope's Road/Station Road
London SW9

The Camden Markets
Off Camden High Street/Chalk Farm Road
Camden
London NW1

Greenwich Market
Greenwich
London SE10

Petticoat Lane Market
(Monday to Friday 10am–2:30pm,
Sunday 9am–2pm)
Middlesex Street
and Wentworth Street
Aldgate
London E1

Portobello Road Market
(Friday and Saturday 8am–3pm)
Portobello Road
London W11

Spitalfield Market
(Monday to Friday [Thursday is vintage]
11am–5pm, Sunday 10am–5pm)
Commercial Street
London E1

New York markets

Artists and Fleas
(Saturday and Sunday)
33 Tenth Avenue
Manhattan, NY

Brooklyn Flea
(Saturday and Sunday)
One Hanson Place
Brooklyn, NY

Green Flea Markets
(Sunday)
100 West 77th Street
New York, NY 10024

Hester Street Fair
(Saturday)
Seward Park, Lower East Side
New York, NY

The Market NYC
159 Bleecker Street
New York, NY 10012

Williamsburg Flea Market
(Sunday)
Wythe Avenue
Brooklyn, NY

Young Designers Market
(Wednesday to Sunday)
159 Bleecker Street
Manhattan, NY

Paris markets

Des Fille en Aiguille
(March–May)
28, rue Beaurepaine
75010
Paris

Le Coutique Ephémère
(Every two months)
Galerie Joseph
7 Rue Froissant, 3rd
Paris

Saint-Ouen
Le Marché Rétro d'Oberkampf
(One Saturday per month)
57 rue Condorcet
Paris

St-Ouen Flea Market
Marché aux Puces
93400
Paris

Shops and markets

Suppliers

London

Alma Leather
(Leather)
12–14 Greatorex Street
London E1 5NF
www.almahome.co.uk

The Bead Shop
(Beads)
21a Tower Street
London WC2H 9NS
www.beadshop.co.uk

Bennett Silks
(Silk)
Crown Royal Park
Higher Hillgate
Stockport SK1 3EY
www.bennett-silks.co.uk

Bernstein and Banleys
(Lining)
Unit 7, Britannia Business Park
Comet Way
Southend-on-Sea
Essex SS2 6GE
www.qualitylinings.co.uk

The Berwick Street Cloth Shop
(Large selection of fabrics)
14 Berwick St
London W1F 0PP
www.theberwickstreetclothshop.com

Borovicks
(Fabrics)
16 Berwick Street
London W1F 0HP
www.borovickfabricsltd.co.uk

The Button Queen
(Buttons)
76 Marylebone Lane
London W1U 2PR
www.thebuttonqueen.co.uk

Classic Textiles
44 Goldhawk Road
London W12 8Dh
www.classictextiles.com

The Cloth House
(Fabrics)
Berwick Street
London
www.clothhouse.com

Creative Beadcraft
(Beads and sequins)
20 Beak Street
London W1F 9RE
www.creativebeadcraft.co.uk

Crescent Trading Wool
(Suitings/dress fabrics)
Unit 2 Quaker Court
41 Quaker Street
London E1 6SN
www.crescenttrading.com

Ditto Fabrics
(Fabric shop and online sales)
21 Kensington Gardens
Brighton BN1 4AL
www.dittofabrics.co.uk

Dormeuil
(Luxury cloth and fabric)
35 Sackville Street
London W1S 3EG
0207 439 3723
www.dormeuil.com

Hang Zhou Silks
3 Station Approach
Stoneleigh
Epsom
Surrey KT19 0QZ
www.hangzhousilks.co.uk

Henry Bertrand Ltd
52 Holmes Road
Kentish Town
NW5 3AB
www.henrybertrand.co.uk

Holland and Sherry
(Suitings)
9–10 Saville Row
London W1S 3PF
www.hollandandsherry.co.uk

James Hare
(Silk merchants)
Monarch House
Queens Street
Leeds LS1 1LX
www.james-hare.com

Joel & Son
(Luxury European prints)
73–83 Church Street
London NW8 8EU
www.joelandsonfabrics.com

John Lewis
(Fabrics and haberdashery)
Oxford Street
London W1
www.johnlewis.com

Joshua Ellis
(Wool suitings)
Grange Road
Batley WF17 6LW
www.joshuaellis.co.uk

J T Batchelor & Co. Ltd
(Leather)
9–10 Culford Mews
Islington
London N1 4DZ
www.jtbatchelor.co.uk

Laurent Garigue
(Fabrics)
68 Pembroke Rd
London W8 6WX
0207 371 1777

Litmans Ltd
(Lace and dress net)
Damad House
490 Radford Road
New Basford
Nottingham
NG7 7EE
www.litmans.org

MacCulloch and Wallis
(Fabrics, linings, and haberdashery)
25–26 Dering Street
London W1S 1AT
www.macculloch-wallis.co.uk

Misan Textiles
(Fine European textiles)
4 Berwick Street
London W1F ODR
www.misan.co.uk

New Rainbow Textiles
(Sari, bridal, silk, and cotton)
98 The Broadway
Southall
Middlesex UB1 1QF

Norman Lyons & Co Ltd
(General fabric shop)
106 Cleveland Street
London W1T 6NX

New York

France

Pongees
(Silk)
28–30 Hoxton Square
London N1 6NN
www.pongees.co.uk

Schwarzschild Ochs
(Fabrics)
210 Great Portland Street
London W1W 5BQ
www.schwarzschildochs.co.uk

**S & K Leather Goods
and Fittings**
436 Essex Road
London N1 3QP
www.skfittings.co.uk

Soho Silks
(General fabrics)
22 D'Arblay Street
London W1F 8ED
www.sohosilks.co.uk

Trade Eighty
(Silk)
Studland Hall
Studland Street
London W6 0JS
www.trade80silks.co.uk

Whaley's (Bradford) Ltd
(Fabric)
Harris Court
Great Horton
Bradford BD7 4EQ
www.whaleys-bradford.ltd.uk

What the Butler Wore
(Vintage clothing and accessories)
131 Lower Marsh
London SE1
www.whatthebutlerwore.co.uk

William Gee
(Haberdashery and linings)
522 Kingsland Rd
London E8 4AR
www.williamgee.co.uk

Berenstein Textiles
(Bridal, evening wear, high fashion,
performance, linings, wool, silk)
270 West 39th Street, 20th floor
New York, NY 10018
www.berensteintextiles.com

C + J Textiles
(Silk)
230 West 38th Street, 7th floor
New York, NY 10018

Eatontex Resources Ltd.
(Acrylic and acrylic blends)
11 Penn Plaza, 5th floor
New York, NY
www.eatontexresources.com

**Garment Industry
Development Corp.**
(Fabric and training)
262 West 38th Street, Suite 506
New York, NY
www.fashionsourceny.com

Natasha International, Inc.
(Cotton, cotton blends, linen, silk)
226 West 37th Street, 7th floor
New York, NY
www.natashafabrics.com

Deltex
(Trimmings, embroidery, tulle, leather
threads)
Route De Souillac
24200 Sarlat
France

Motif Personnel
98, rue de Verdun
92270 Bois Colombes
France
www.motifpersonnel.com

Sodertex
(Cords, strings, ribbons, ropes)
14 Rue Rémi Moïse
42150 La Ricamarie
France
www.sodertex.com

Textile Service J. M.
(Linen, cotton, silk)
16 rue des Jardines
8110 Burlats
France
www.textile-service-jm.fr

Les Trouvailles D'amandine
(Organic fabric)
3 Grange Allée Le Nôtre 77185
Lognes
France
www.lestrouvaillesdamandine.com/en

Fashion weeks, trade shows, and fabric fairs

UK fashion weeks

British Fashion Council
www.londonfashionweek.co.uk

Scoop International Fashion Show
www.scoop-international.com

US fashion weeks

Bridal Fashion Week
www.couturefashionweek.com

Council of Fashion Designers of America
www.cfda.com

Los Angeles Fashion Week
www.fashionweekla.com

New York Fashion Week
www.mbfashionweek.com

European fashion weeks

Copenhagen Fashion Week
www.copenhagenfashionweek.com

Ethical Fashion Show
www.ethicalfashionshowberlin.com

Mercedes-Benz Berlin Fashion Week
www.fashionweek-berlin.mercedes-benz.de

Mercedes-Benz Madrid Fashion Week
www.ifema.es/mercedesbenzfwm_06

Milan
www.cameramoda.it

Paris Fashion Week
www.modeaparis.com

Stockholm Fashion Week
www.stockholmfashionweek.com

Valencia Fashion Week
www.valenciafashionweek.com

Australian fashion weeks

Australia Fashion Week
http://australiafashionweeklive.com

L'Oréal Melbourne Fashion Festival
www.lmff.com.au

Mercedes-Benz Fashion Festival Brisbane
www.mbff.com.au

Mercedes-Benz Rosemount Sydney Fashion
Festival
www.mbffsydney.com.au

Perth Fashion Festival
www.telstraperthfashionfestival.com.au

Trade shows and fabric fairs

Apparelsourcing
www.apparelsourcingshow.com

Copenhagen International Fashion Fair
www.ciff.dk

Interstoff
www.interstoff-asia.com

Linea Pelle
www.lineapelle-fair.it

Messe Frankfurt
www.messefrankfurt.com

Pitti Filati
www.pittimmagine.com

Prèmiere Vision
www.premiervision.fr

Rendez-Vous Paris
www.rendez-vous-paris.com

Tissu Premier
www.tissu-premier.com

Fashion journals, museums, and blogs

Fashion journals

10
A Magazine
Acne
Another Magazine
Another Man
Arts Thread (print and online)
Cliché
Complex
Crash
Dazed and Confused
Eco-textile News (print and online)
Encens
Fantastic Man
Fashion Practice (online only)
Fashion Theory (online only)
GQ Style
The Gentlewoman
Grazia
Harper's Bazaar (UK and US)
i-D
International Journal of Fashion Design, Technology, and Education
Jocks & Nerds (online only)
L'Officiel
Love
Lucky
Lulu
Marie Claire
Monocle (print and online)
Numero
Nylon
Pop
Purple
Self Service
Sleek
So-en
Tank
Textile (online only)
Textile View
Vogue (Casa, English, Hommes, Italia, Paris, Uomo, US)
W Magazine

UK museums

Design Museum
www.designmuseum.org

Fashion and Textile Museum
www.ftm.org

The Gallery in Redchurch Street
www.galleryinredchurchstreet.com

The Hayward Gallery
www.haywardgallery.org.uk

Hunterian Museum
http://www.gla.ac.uk/hunterian

Imperial War Museum
www.iwm.org.uk

The Museum of Everything
www.museumofeverything.com

Royal Academy of Arts
www.royalacademy.org.uk

Serpentine Gallery
www.serpentinegallery.org

Saatchi Gallery
www.saatchi-gallery.co.uk

Tate Modern
www.tate.org.uk/modern

Victoria and Albert
www.vam.ac.uk

The Wapping Project
www.thewappingproject.com

The Wellcome Collection
http://wellcomelibrary.org

US museums

The Black Fashion Museum Collection (Smithsonian)
Washington, DC
www.nmaahc.si.edu/collections/blackfashion

**The Costume Institute
(The Metropolitan Museum of Art)**
New York
http://www.metmuseum.org/about-the-museum/museum-
departments/curatorial-departments/
the-costume-institute

Fashion and Art Gallery
www.faag.us

**The Museum at FIT
(Fashion Institute of Technology)**
New York
www.fitnyc.edu/museum.asp

European museums

Les Arts Décoratifs
Paris, France
www.lesartsdecoratifs.fr

The Balenciaga Museum
Getaria, Spain
http://cristobalbalenciagamuseoa.com

The Gucci Museum
Florence, Italy
www.guccimuseo.com

Mode Museum
Antwerp, Belgium
www.momu.be

Musée Galleria
Paris, France
www.palaisgalleria.paris.fr

Museo Salvatore Ferragamo
Florence, Italy
www.ferragamo.com/museo

Tassen Museum Hedrikje
Amsterdam, Netherlands
www.tassenmuseum.nl

Blogs

http://alexdemora.blogspot.com/
http://annatrevelyan.blogspot.com/
http://ashadedviewonfashion.com/
http://blackmaskenterprise.blogspot.com/
http://blogs.colette.fr/colette/
http://blogs.colette.fr/mandi/
http://bybellazine.blogspot.com/
http://cocknbullkid.com/
http://danwilton.blogspot.com/
http://disneyrollergirl.blogspot.com/
http://fleshwig.blogspot.com/
http://fredbutlerstyle.blogspot.com/
http://fuminagasaka.blogspot.com/
http://kimhowells.blogspot.com/
http://kingaburza.tumblr.com/

http://lapinsdancehall.co.uk/
http://livinginmagazines.blogspot.com/
http://makiloulou.blogspot.com/
http://matthewjosephs.blogspot.com/
http://mattirwinlondon.blogspot.com/
http://miniaturelove.blogspot.com/
http://novadando.blogspot.com/
http://plushpatterns.blogspot.com/
http://robotsatbombay.blogspot.com/
http://rorydcs.blogspot.com/
http://showstudio.com/
http://skintings.blogspot.com/
http://stylebubble.typepad.com/
http://theoisamazing.blogspot.com/
http://therealkesh.blogspot.com/
http://theselby.com/
http://thomasdekluyver.blogspot.com/
http://www.alexanderliang.com/
http://www.alwaysjudging.com/
http://www.ameliasmagazine.com/
http://www.anothermag.com/reader/
http://www.ashley-ringmybell.blogspot.fr/
http://www.brooklynblonde.com/
http://www.charlielemindu.com/mag/
http://www.closetfreaksblog.com/
http://www.dailyrubbish.co.uk/
http://www.dapperlou.com/journal/
http://www.dazeddigital.com/
http://www.deluneblog.com/
http://www.eleykishimoto.com/blog/
http://www.fashion156.com/blog.php/
http://www.hintmag.com/blog/blog.php/
http://www.iamgalla.com/
http://www.igobyfrankie.com/
http://www.itsnicethat.com/
http://www.itssuperfashion.com/
http://www.joesafiend.blogspot.com/
http://www.katelovesme.net/
http://www.katwalksf.com/
http://www.le21eme.com/
http://www.le-happy.com/
http://www.lfwdaily.com/
http://www.manrepeller.com/
http://www.marcelokrasilcic.blogspot.com/
http://www.Matthewstone.co.uk/
http://www.nicolaformichetti.blogspot.com/
http://www.papermag.com/
http://www.rosynicholas.blogspot.com/
http://www.rowdysuperstar.blogspot.com/
http://www.scottee-scottee.blogspot.com/
http://www.scoutsixteen.com/
http://www.sophyrobson.com/
http://www.spadgerdisco.blogspot.com/
http://www.stylemarmalade.com/
http://www.superchargedamf.blogspot.com/
http://www.thedailynice.com/
http://www.troprouge.blogspot.fr/
http://www.vogue.co.uk/blogs/the-vogue-blog/
http://www.waynetippetts.com/
http://www.weareallinone.blogspot.com/
http://www.weworewhat.com/
http://www.wheredidugetthat.com/
http://youworkit.co.uk/category/blog/

Acknowledgments

With thanks to John Lau and Jennifer Prendergast for their help in reviewing the manuscript in its formative stages, to Helen Stallion for her help in securing the images, and to Sophie Hodgson for her support. The publishers would like to offer special thanks to Colette Meacher and Lucy Tipton. It is with great sadness that we remember Joe Bates of Sibling, who was the most talented, stylish, funny, and inspirational designer and tutor and will be missed by all who knew him.

Picture credits

All reasonable attempts have been made to trace, clear, and credit the copyright holders of the images reproduced in this book. However, if any credits have been inadvertently omitted, the publisher will endeavor to incorporate amendments in future editions.

Cover image: Zoe Wells, Kingston University Collection line up 2014.

Introduction

1. Lucinda Popp, 2. Mitchell Sams.

Chapter 1

1. Mitchell Sams, 2. Mitchell Sams, 3. Getty, 4. Michael Woolley, 5. Mitchell Sams, 6. ©Meyerwiel.com 2014, 7. Poppy Dover, 8. Poppy Dover, 9. Mitchell Sams, 10. Dimitrios Kambouris/Getty, 11. N/A, 12. Lucinda Popp, 13. Lucinda Popp, 14. LS:N Global (the trends and insight arm of The Future Laboratory) design direction story. ©The Future Laboratory, photography by Richard Install, 15. Compiling research at The Future Laboratory. ©The Future Laboratory, photography by Richard Install, 16. Holly Berry, 17. Jens Laugesen Studio, 18. Reg Lancaster/Getty, 19. E. Tautz team: Patrick Grant, Ikla Wright, Felix Chabluk Smith, 20. E. Tautz team: Patrick Grant, Ikla Wright, Felix Chabluk Smith, 21. E. Tautz team: Patrick Grant, Ikla Wright, Felix Chabluk Smith, 22. Getty, 23. Mitchell Sams, 24. Shelley Fox, 25. Art direction and graphic designer: Hem Patel; photographer: Willem Jaspert; stylist: Jason Hughes; designer: Satyenkumar Patel, 26. Mitchell Sams, 27. Mitchell Sams, 28. Mitchell Sams, 29. The Future Laboratory Yard, London. ©The Future Laboratory, photography by Richard Install, 30. Shelley Fox. Photography by Chris Moore and styling by Jane Howard, 31. Todd Lynn, 32. Todd Lynn, 33. Richard Nicoll, 34. Richard Nicoll, 35. Felipe Rojas Llanos.

Chapter 2

1. Mitchell Sams, 2. Mitchell Sams, 3. Pierre Verdy/AFP/Getty Images, 4. Rolls Press/ Popperfoto/Getty Images, 5. Mitchell Sams, 6. Francois Guilot/ AFP/Getty Images, 7. Mitchell Sams, 8. NBCU Photo Bank/Getty, 9. Dan Kitwood/Getty Images, 10. Sinead Lynch/AFP/Getty Images, 11. Mitchell Sams, 12. Simon Dawson/ Bloomberg via Getty Images, 13. Mitchell Sams, 14. Michael Woolley, 15. Peter Perret, 16. Mitchell Sams, 17. Mitchell Sams, 18. Courtesy of the London College of Fashion and The Woolmark Company, 19. Mitchell Sams, 20. Mitchell Sams, 21. Photographer:

Morgan White; stylist: Kim Howells; hair: Amiee Robinson; makeup: Mel Arter @ CLM; model: Emma C @ IMG, 22. Photographer: Morgan White; stylist: Kim Howells; hair: Amiee Robinson; makeup: Mel Arter @ CLM; model: Emma C @ IMG, 23. Sophie Hulme, 24. Kenneth MacKenzie, 25. Will Broome, 26. Will Broome, 27. Will Broome.

Chapter 3

1. Mitchell Sams, 2. London College of Fashion, 3. Mitchell Sams, 4. Wesley/Keystone/Getty Images, 5. Mitchell Sams, 6. Mitchell Sams, 7. Mitchell Sams, 8. Mitchell Sams, 9. Images used with courtesy of M&S, 10. Images permission of Giles Deacon, 11. Christopher Dadey for Sibling, 12. Arcadia, 13. Photo: Simon Evans, 14. Nicolas Aristidou photographed our SS14. editorial and Julia Bostock our AW13. editorial.

Chapter 4

1. Mitchell Sams, 2. Christopher Dadey for Sibling, 3. © Charli Cohen. Photography by Andre Regini, 4. Tom's Kitchen photography by Nick Dunne, 5. Nicholas Kirkwood Ltd, 6. Caramel Baby & Child, 7. Caramel Baby & Child, 8. Caramel Baby & Child, 9. Caramel Baby & Child, 10. Photographer: Amy Gwatkin; stylist: Nell Kalonji, 11. Photographer: Amy Gwatkin; stylist: Nell Kalonji, 12. © Charli Cohen. Photography by Nicole Markhoff, 13. Oliver Ruuger. Photography by Michiel Meewis, 14. Oliver Ruuger. Photography by Alejandro Cavallo.

Chapter 5

1. Designed by Sophie Wetherell. Location: Graduate Fashion Week, 2–4. Stefanie Tschirky, 5. Alex Baldwin, 6. Alex Baldwin, 7. Camille Hardwick, 8. Camille Hardwick, 9. Camille Hardwick, 10. Camille Hardwick, 11–12. Anna Yates, 13. Krista Hendriksen, 14. Krista Hendriksen, 15. Héléna Denize, 16. Héléna Denize, 17. Jean Philippe Chemin, 18. Jean Philippe Chemin, 19. Krista Hendriksen, 20. Simon Armstrong, 21. Lauren Lake, 22. Sadie Clayton, 23. Collection by Phoebe Kowalska. Photography by Will Corry, 24. Collection by Phoebe Kowalska. Photography by Will Corry, 25. Amy Heath, 26. Simon Armstrong.